WILMETTE PUBLIC LIBRARY

3 1239 00777 9769

D0822311

The Rogue's Road to Retirement

WITHDRAWN
Wilmette Public Library

Wilmette Public Library
1242 Wilmette Avenue
Wilmette, Il 60091
847-256-5025

The Rogue's Road to Retirement

How I Got My Groove Back after Sixty-Five—and How You Can, Too!

George S. K. Rider

Skyhorse Publishing

WILMETTE PUBLIC LIBRARY

Copyright © 2015 by George S. K. Rider

All rights reserved. No part of this book may be reproduced in any manner without the express written consent of the publisher, except in the case of brief excerpts in critical reviews or articles. All inquiries should be addressed to Skyhorse Publishing, 307 West 36th Street, 11th Floor, New York, NY 10018.

Skyhorse Publishing books may be purchased in bulk at special discounts for sales promotion, corporate gifts, fund-raising, or educational purposes. Special editions can also be created to specifications. For details, contact the Special Sales Department, Skyhorse Publishing, 307 West 36th Street, 11th Floor, New York, NY 10018 or info@skyhorsepublishing.com.

Skyhorse® and Skyhorse Publishing® are registered trademarks of Skyhorse Publishing, Inc.®, a Delaware corporation.

Visit our website at www.skyhorsepublishing.com.

10 9 8 7 6 5 4 3 2 1

Library of Congress Cataloging-in-Publication Data is available on file.

Cover design by Qualcom Design

Print ISBN: 978-1-62914-766-6

Ebook ISBN: 978-1-63220-110-2

Printed in the United States of America

646.79
RI

For

Dorothy, my wonderful wife and partner for
fifty great and exciting years; our son, Graham;
his wife, Paulette; and their children,
Graham Jr., Bradley, Victoria, and Duncan;
and our daughter, Jennifer; and her husband,
William McKeever.

B.T 1/6/15

Contents

Contents

Contents

Introduction

Throw away your cardigan, your practical shoes, your fish oil pills, and Maalox. There's much more to life after retirement than playing golf and looking after the grandkids. Get back in touch with your inner rascal and get going.

Every day, eight thousand Baby Boomers across the U.S. turn sixty-five[1] and start the rollercoaster ride into retirement, joining the thirty-eight million who are already retired.[2] This is a journey that can all too often become filled with empty days, boredom, and loneliness, as older Americans struggle to redefine and re-launch themselves.

I say "just say no" to slowing down and growing stodgy! I've written *The Rogue's Road to Retirement* for all you rebels, raconteurs, and roués out there (you know who you are!)

---

[1] AARP http://www.aarp.org/personal-growth/transitions/boomers_65/

[2] Social Security Administration http://www.ssa.gov/news/press/basic-fact.html

who don't want to grow old gracefully . . . who want to grow old the way you grew up—raising hell and having fun.

I am an eighty-two-year-old husband, father, and grandfather who has traveled a colorful (and mischievous) path after retirement and become an avowed believer in the philosophy that—with the right attitude and the right game plan—you can prevent yourself from becoming yet another aging, cranky, overweight couch potato. In fact, I believe you can make your retirement years the best—and the most fun and meaningful—time of your life. My advice? Follow the three Rs:

- Recharge Your Batteries. Get off your duff, get a new passion, and get back in the game. You were never boring before you turned sixty or seventy. Why start now?
- Record Your Memories. Write down your greatest hits for your grandchildren and the generations beyond, and not just your moments of glory, but also your moments of mischief-making. Let's face it! They're the ones you're most proud of anyway!
- Revel in What Should and Can be the Best Time of Your Life. Reflect, make peace with growing older, and make the most of each day.

Told through a series of madcap adventures (think Mr. Magoo meets a graying, leather-clad Malcolm Forbes on his motorcycle), *The Rogue's Road to Retirement* is designed to inspire seniors everywhere to keep trying new things until you find your passion. In my case, that's meant landing a part in a TV commercial for Pepsi doing the polka, starring in an MTV video with folk rock artist Joan Osborne, and swanning around writers' conferences throughout my seventies and eighties, among other geriatric flights of fancy.

The Rogue's Road to Retirement will also show you how to take stock of your fondest memories and defining moments, celebrate your youthful indiscretions, and reclaim the bad boy or girl within.

Finally, *The Rogue's Road to Retirement* will help you to reflect on, and savor, the sweetness of growing older, which can include such victories as always getting a parking spot after you've finally succumbed to getting a handicap sticker; holding your grandchild for the first time and reveling in the fact that you are no longer the baldest member of your family; watching in amazement as your kids take you out to dinner—and actually pick up the tab for the first time in their lives; and being able to ignore people anytime you feel like it just by pretending you're hard of hearing. *What did you say? Sorry, I can't hear you!*

The Rogue's Road to Retirement is about looking back while pushing forward. It's a funny, poignant, universal guide to retirement and aging—dedicated to anyone like you or me who won't give up and won't grow old without a fight.

Chapter 1

The Second Stage of No—Surviving Turning Seventy

The Second Stage of No! When I neared seventy more than a decade ago, I was rudely awakened by a new set of rules. Not since I was a child were there so many dos and don'ts. With a hip replacement operation looming, a physical scheduled every twelve weeks, regular eye check-ups for glaucoma, skin cancer harvests at least twice a year, and a PSA check every six months, I was constantly being told to pop pills, drip drops, lose weight, exercise, and not drink. (OK, maybe I cheated a bit on the last one.) The list seemed endless. Dorothy, my ever-loving wife, became the enforcer.

A few weeks before the big day, my seventieth birthday, my right eye began to blur. I had to face the music. I made an appointment to see a specialist in New York City for May 13 at 11:00 a.m., despite my lack of mobility resulting from arthritis in several joints, and a wonky left hip, right knee, and right ankle from various football and skiing mishaps. Walking was and is not a pretty sight for me most days.

At the time, 9/11 was still laser sharp in everyone's memories, and the thought of traveling forty-eight miles into the city for any reason was daunting. All of my working life—more than four and half decades—had been spent commuting to Wall Street before sunrise on the Long Island Railroad. Now retired, I viewed the trek as a necessary, but giant, imposition. Excuses for putting off my eye check-up were easy . . . procrastination the order du jour.

When the dreaded day arrived, Dorothy dropped me off to catch the jitney into the city and reminded me to behave, keep my eye (the good one) on the time, and come right home after the appointment as we had a dinner date that night. The traffic was light, and there was no stress, other than my nagging need to hit the men's room. My plumbing had been slightly rearranged during a successful prostate removal at Sloane Kettering, so anything over an hour usually became agonizing! Finally, the jitney deposited me at Second Avenue and Seventy-Ninth Street, three doors from the doctor's office. I checked my watch, much more aware of the time than I had ever been before I retired, despite the fact that now I had no real place to go. *Time elapsed: one hour and fifteen minutes.*

Preliminary screening and testing completed, I was ushered into an examination room. Moments later the doctor appeared, reviewed the test data, and proceeded with the exam. I looked down at my watch. *One hour, thirty minutes since departure.*

Not bad, not bad at all, I thought. I'd be home in time for a late lunch. But then the doctor motioned for me to stay seated. We had a few things to discuss.

The news was not good. Not only had the pressure gone up in my right eye, my left eye was also diagnosed with glaucoma. Our discussion was followed by a gentle but firm lecture on follow-up discipline (it had been over a year since my last appointment). I left kicking myself. Although the condition could be treated, I had taken an unnecessary risk by delaying my appointment, and the disease could still compromise my eyesight if I wasn't more careful. I was shaken by the news.

I exited the office armed with two new eye drop prescriptions and decided to take the train home to Long Island. I hailed a cab. The day was overcast and dreary, the traffic snarled, and my pupils dilated. "Penn Station, please!" On the way across town, I reflected. In a few days, I'd be seventy. I had glaucoma in both eyes, a skin condition, a blood pressure condition, a cholesterol condition, no prostate, and constant underlying pain that radiated every which way when it rained. Just then it started to rain. As my son liked to say, "Dad, if you were a horse, they'd shoot you!"

"Cabby, take me to 44th and Vanderbilt instead," I implored, knocking insistently on the plastic partition. To hell with Penn Station! The doctor's admonitions were fading fast! The driver turned around and sped off to the Yale Club, my home away from home during my working days.

At least I'd get to see some of my old buddies. I hadn't been to the Yale Club since the previous summer. Much to my chagrin, the new second floor bartender informed me that his predecessor Ozzie had, after twenty-five years of fine service and friendship, retired the previous year. The new bartender also informed me that one of my old pals had died suddenly (heart attack), one was recently admitted to a hospital uptown (liver flapping from cirrhosis caused by a lifetime of single-malt Scotch and steak), and another was so crippled with arthritis that he rarely came in. This news added to my malaise.

I quickly ordered a short glass of amber liquid over ice for fortification and headed to the computer monitor in the hallway to check the market, drink in hand. The color red accompanied all of my ticker symbols. My mood now matched the lousy weather. I'd seen enough and moved to the lounge, grabbing the *New York Times* sports section (the only part worth reading in that paper anymore, in my opinion) from the table. I settled into one of the comfortable, oversized, overstuffed chairs. I'd check the Stanley Cup results, finish my drink, and be off. *No need to feel guilty*, I told myself. *It's not like anyone's watching.*

The adult beverage temporarily alleviated my dour mood, but just temporarily. *Elapsed time: two hours, thirty minutes, or so I thought—my eyes still blurred from the doctor's drops.*

I hailed another cab for Penn Station. The driver was a talkative young guy from Lebanon. I told him of my experiences there in 1956 as a young Navy Lieutenant Junior Grade (j.g.) visiting Beirut on a destroyer. As I reminisced about the ancient city of Baalbek, the belly dancers, the Kit Kat Club, and the beautiful beaches, I found my mood starting to improve. Dorothy had given me $63 in the a.m. I'd spent $18 on the jitney, $8 on the first cab, another $8 or so on the second taxi, so I figured I should have plenty left for a slice of pizza at Penn Station. When I reached into my pocket to pay the driver, I pulled out four singles. God knows where I lost the balance. The meter read $7.50. What should I do? (This was back before NYC taxis accepted credit cards.) I told the cabby, "It's been a bad day. I'm losing sight in one eye." This was a slight exaggeration, but desperate times require desperate measures. "I'll be seventy this week, and I've somehow lost all my money. Please give me your address, and I'll send you the balance."

He responded, "No. Not necessary. Please remember just because of 9/11 not all Arabs aren't bad. I've enjoyed this conversation, I'm from Beirut!"

Armed with an American Express card and otherwise empty pockets, I exited the cab. The "Hall of Fame" bar in the basement of the LIRR terminal across from the track beckoned.

I worked out a game plan: I'd order a drink, overpay the chit on my Am Ex by $10.00, add a handsome tip, ask for the difference in cash so I could pay my train fare, and be on my way. I ordered a drink from the gruff but familiar bartender and explained my strategy. "We don't do that anymore. By the way, there's a minimum credit card purchase!" Now I had a drink, an open tab, and still no money. The bartender chimed in, "Try the ATM machine five store fronts down."

"Great." I limped down to the machine, dragging my left leg behind me. The store guard came to the rescue, but nothing worked. "What's your PIN number?" he asked. How should I know? What's a PIN number? "I don't use these things—my wife only gave it to me for emergencies." Another failed mission!

I did a "walk of shame" back to the "Hall of Fame." The "friendly" bartender advanced me 25 cents. I dialed home to Dorothy on the thirty-second phone. "Hi. Eye news not all good," I stammered. "I somehow lost most of the money. I'll be on the 2:27 p.m. to Bay Shore . . . Have to talk quick."

"What's wrong with your eyes?" Dorothy grilled me. "You lost the money? George? George?!" Thirty seconds were up. Click.

I closed out the Am Ex bill. *Why not use up the minimum?* I thought as I ordered another Scotch. "Make it a double." *Time elapsed: Who knows at this point? All I know is, I want to go home.*

I headed for the train. I'd missed the 2:27 p.m. With no change in my pocket, there was no way to call home again. I hobbled onto the 3:10 p.m. on track eighteen. The pushcart bartender on the platform recognized me. "Long time no see. How's retirement?"

I thought quickly, "Well, I'll be seventy on Thursday . . ."

"Oh, you better have this." He handed me a gin and tonic, saying, "Happy Birthday. Don't be a stranger. Great to see you."

I boarded the train with empty pockets, a G&T, and the *New York Times* sports section I purloined from the Yale Club lounge and chose a one-seater at the far end of the car. Before long, the conductor made his way up the aisle. He was a tall, pleasant-looking, middle-aged guy in a neat uniform, well-groomed and efficient. Before he could ask for my ticket, I blurted out, "This has been a terrible day. I'll be seventy the day after tomorrow, my eye doctor just told me that I am going blind in both eyes (I built upon my earlier exaggeration), I'm arthritic in three joints, I've lost all my money, I'll gladly pay by credit card . . ." I rattled on.

The conductor interrupted me. "Are you Irish, Red?"

"Yes."

"Happy Birthday. When you change at Jamaica, go to the last car and ask for Ray. Tell him Jim said you're okay. He's a good friend. You should be fine." My luck had changed, finally.

At Jamaica, Ray was nowhere to be found. Instead, there was a thin, grumpy-looking female conductor walking up the aisle like she was on a mission. The way most of the day had gone, they'd probably stop the train and throw me off at Massapequa, the next stop. She somehow sensed my anxiety and asked if everything was okay. I proceeded to relate my now well-rehearsed and increasingly embroidered tale of woe (from treatable glaucoma to tin cup and cane in less than four hours). I worked up the nerve and was just about to ask her if she knew Jim or Ray when she looked at me knowingly and said, "Take care of your eyes, Sugar, and take care of yourself." She patted me on the cheek like I was a baby or a blank-eyed nursing home patient. Still, I was one step closer to home.

One more hurdle to go. I checked my watch again. The numbers on the dial were still fuzzy from my dilated eyes (and the G&T!). Dorothy had now been waiting an extra thirty minutes—or was it fifty? The train stopped. I spotted the old Buick station wagon with my long-suffering wife at the wheel. I blended in with the crowd so she wouldn't see me stumble, circled around the rear of the car, and gingerly opened the passenger door, ready to launch into my now memorized litany of aging woes. Luck once again prevailed. Dorothy was too concerned about my eyes to ask me where the hell I'd been. The thorough debriefing about my afternoon adventures would take place at a later date. For now, I was home at last. Thank God.

So, you see, the Second Stage of No hasn't been so bad, after all, and turning seventy—and even eighty—hasn't been as traumatic as I expected. (In fact, now that I'm eighty-two and counting, seventy seems positively jejune.)

Current time elapsed: Eighty-two years, eight months!

Chapter 2

Old Dogs, New Tricks? Finding a Raison d'Être in Retirement

I retired from Wall Street in 1995 in my mid-sixties and immediately became clutter in my own house. The animals had a hard time adjusting. My wife seemed to be everywhere. I'd come down in the morning and find our cats Willie and Charlie asleep on both chairs in the den. Rosie, our Heinz '57 poodle-terrier-whatever-look-alike, lay sprawled on the couch. It took a little doing, but I'd finally dislodge one of them and settle down, coffee within reach, remote in hand, paper at the ready. Peace at last—at least for a few brief moments. But then my reverie would be interrupted by the sound of the dreaded vacuum cleaner propelled by a stern-faced wife determined to eradicate every trace of me. Was this my house, or was I just a guest? *Does this go on every day?* I wondered.

My frequent suggestions and ideas on improved efficiency—a better way to stack the dishes and sort cupboards, for example, or a strategically revamped schedule for shopping, cleaning, and trips to bank and dry cleaner—all fell on deaf ears. This wasn't Wall Street. I wasn't in charge. Keeping busy became the order of the day. I volunteered for several boards, the chamber of commerce, and the business improvement district. I also chaired the redevelopment committee of downtown Bay Shore, our then-hometown on Long Island. I even tried my hand at elective office, unseating the incumbent Lonelyville, Fire Island Fire Commissioner in a resounding thumping: twenty-one votes for me, six votes for him. This was quite an honor, since the four-street-wide town where we spend our summers has no firehouse and no fire-fighting equipment (we lease from neighboring Fair Harbor). However, I had a shiny new badge to show for my victory, which was a big hit with my four young grandchildren.

My existence became very sterile. I was again unfulfilled, as I had been during my days as a trader. "Time on My Hands" became my theme song. I had to do something.

Trump I Wasn't

A friend of mine in real estate suggested that I take the licensing exam and join her firm. I put the decision off for several weeks, discussed it with Dorothy, and decided to give it a try. I signed up for the course and started classes. This should be easy compared to Wall Street. How hard could it be? Plus, I'd make some bucks along the way. Don't kid yourself as I did. To do it right, you need courses in survival and hand-to-hand combat to go along with the certificate.

The local real estate scene was dominated by schools of tough, ferociously smart young women who were superhumanly working while raising families and volunteering on multiple boards and committees—all without breaking a sweat. I fondly called them "piranhas in pumps," a phrase I am sure they would have considered a compliment. This group was not about to make room willingly for a part-time, power-grabbing male retiree.

I completed the course and was given a desk at one of the more successful brokerages in our area. I meet people easily—conversation has never been a problem for me—and I had years of experience in sales. I took readily to my new pursuit.

I got off to a fast start with four big listings in the first six weeks. The paperwork and the handholding of clients didn't bother me, but splitting the first five commissions with my trainer did. The broker also took a cut. After a short while, associating day to day with the "piranhas" and watching my hard-earned commission checks slashed into pieces took its toll.

To make matters worse, shortly after starting my new endeavor, I was diagnosed with prostate cancer and operated on at Sloane Kettering five months later. The third day after the seven-hour operation, I was lying in my hospital bed, still groggy from the morphine, when the phone rang. I fumbled for it.

"Hello, George. This is Gretchen (name changed to protect the guilty). How are you doing? Remember your listing on Plymouth East Street? I sold it for you, partner." As sick and woozy as I felt, I knew the word "partner" could only mean trouble. My instinct proved to be correct. Gretchen took half my listing commission and the whole commission from her side of the transaction. It occurred to me that if I had died on the table, it would have simplified the paperwork, and she could have had all the money. I'm sure that thought crossed her mind more than once as well!

By the time I had recuperated, the little fish with the big teeth had cannibalized the rest of my listings, and I was forced to share more income with those who had little or nothing to do with producing it. "Team" was a word foreign to their vocabulary. The real estate scene left me cold; Donald Trump I wasn't. I didn't work all my life to hate what I was doing in retirement. Plus, I knew I had dodged a bullet. Although my PSA was back to zero, I had no desire to waste precious time with the piranhas. Besides, as I soon realized, I had other fish to fry.

Lights, Camera, Action!

A storm-tossed late-August trip on the ferry to Fire Island planted the seed for my next big post-retirement adventure. There I was, sharing the rain-drenched top deck with an attractive redhead. The weather was so bad that her husband wasn't there to greet her. The best course of action, of course, was to ride out the storm at the one bar in town, where I ordered a pitcher of margaritas.

"What do you do?" Nancy asked me from across the table.

"I'm retired."

"You have a distinctive look. Did you ever think about doing commercials?"

"Who, me?" Her question surprised me. I was flattered, but I didn't show it. "I'm an ex-jock. Art galleries and museums are not my bag. I don't even think I know what 'creative' means!"

Our verbal joust continued. We soon realized we were neighbors, with nearby cottages in our little village of Lonelyville. I suggested we arrange a dinner with our respective spouses. We swapped names and numbers. The weather cleared, so we drained the pitcher and departed for our homes.

Several days later, the phone rang. "George, this is Nancy. Take down this number. My friend Anne is a professional photographer. Get your headshots done. I'll help you with the agents."

After a near seven-decade drought, my creative juices had begun to flow.

The next morning I called Anne and made an appointment to meet her the following Tuesday at her apartment on Central Park West. She suggested that I wear a light blue or white open neck sports shirt, jeans or chinos, and a light sweater. She also asked me to bring a dark blue business suit, button down shirt, and a regimental tie.

When I arrived at her apartment, Anne offered me a cup of coffee and proceeded to outline the shoot. It would entail two different sessions, one with me in sports clothes and one in business attire, taken at several locations in the park.

Anne gathered her cameras and tote bag filled with extra film, water bottles, and wipes. I picked up my suit bag. We left the apartment and headed for the park across the street from her building. The time was mid-August, the temperature was ninety degrees, and the air was heavy and steamy. Fortunately, the first location was in a shady area with a large rock in the background. Anne posed me in several positions, suggesting attitudes, some serious, and some smiling. We talked as she clicked. We moved to a higher, more open spot that was rocky with no underbrush, and then finally to an open field. At each location the posing, coaching, and clicking were repeated. Anne knew her stuff.

After about an hour, we took a break. Anne handed me a towel and wipes for my face and water to drink. There I sat, shirt off, with sweat from my brow and shoulders rolling down over my abdominal protuberance, which was once washboard firm. Chippendales was certainly not an option for me now.

I dried off and changed into my white shirt and tie, combing my hair using a mirror that Anne provided. Several gawkers appeared, and I found myself playing to the crowd with visions of the red carpet dancing through my mind.

We retraced our steps using the same locations in reverse for another hour of posing and clicking. Finally Anne said, "George, that's it. We're done."

A week later, the proofs arrived by registered mail, ninety-six of them to be exact, with a note from Anne suggesting that Dorothy and I select two, one of me in sports clothes, the other in the business suit. The winnowing process took three days. I was already beginning to feel like a star.

True to her word, Nancy provided me with the phone number of a photo shop uptown on Sixth Avenue for the copies and enlargements, and a copy of the Ross Report, which is an alphabetical listing of theatrical agencies and agents.

A week later, armed with a hundred copies of each pose and a list of suggested agents, I busied myself stuffing twenty manila envelopes with headshots and handwritten notes asking for help as a newcomer to the industry.

Soon after, I was in New York for a meeting and decided to hand deliver one of the envelopes to an agent nearby. Direct contact between aspiring actors and agents is a definite no-no, but I decided to do it anyway. I wondered what a real, live agent looked like and accepted the risk.

I rang the bell. The office was uptown on the West Side. Much to my surprise, the owner greeted me warmly, introduced himself, and thanked me for dropping by. Beginner's luck!

By the time I got home that night, the agent had called and left a message. "George, I have an audition for you. Report to Studio 5 at 5:30 p.m. tomorrow. Confirm by phone before 10:00 p.m. Dress in casual working clothes. You will be trying for the part of a cook in a fast food restaurant."

I was flabbergasted. I didn't get the part, but a routine began to unfold involving long lines of actors trying for the same gig, slating (where actors identify themselves on camera and give the names of their agencies), short auditions, some with lines to read or memorize, a lot of waiting, and ample doses of rejection.

More auditions followed for various parts, including a bartender, an army sergeant, a policeman. All I had to show for it was one callback. My years on Wall Street were good preparation for the rejection that followed. But as long as I was learning, the time and effort were worth it.

One dreary December morning, the phone rang. "Hi George, it's Suzy." I had somehow landed not one but three agents by this point. "Can you make a 4:30 p.m. call? Dress casual. You'll be trying for the part of a football coach. This will be a print commercial for *Sports Illustrated*, if you get it. Good luck."

I felt good about this one. The studio was on Twenty-First Street near Sixth Avenue. The receptionist buzzed me in and directed me to Studio C. I counted eleven actors facing each other in a hallway outside a closed door. From time to time, the door opened and a no-nonsense woman named Penelope appeared with a clipboard for signing in. I filled out my space and handed the clipboard back to her. The door opened again. Out strode two huge guys talking animatedly. One of them glanced at me and said off-handedly, "Hi, coach!" The other one wearing a baseball cap on backward looked directly at Penelope and said out loud, "Penny, looks like we've got our coach."

I was ushered right in. Two attractive young women were standing behind a large camera. Several bright lights were focused on a fold-down chair. A big "X" was marked on the floor with white tape in front of the chair. I was given the following instructions: "George, stand on the 'X,' look into the camera, and say your name. Now turn left. Now right. Now look at me. Smile. Thank you. Good luck!" I soaked up the attention. I was back at Penn Station in under an hour and headed home. The phone rang at about 8:30 p.m.

"George! It's Suzy. Congratulations, coach, you got the part. Monday morning report to Baker's Field, Columbia University." She gave me directions. I was like a kid on Christmas Eve. Stardom became a surging blip on my radarscope.

Monday finally came. Baker's Field in late February can be very cold, particularly when the north wind blows in off the

Hudson. This day was overcast and piles of unmelted snow dotted the field. The wind was chilly and biting. I entered the stadium looking for Cindy, one of the producers. She found me first. I followed her under the stands to an office heated by an electric radiator. The theme of the shoot was a spoof on Gatorade by a competing sports drink called All Sport. The tagline was "Guess what happens to 'ALL' the leftover Gatorade?"

Cindy gave me two sets of everything. I wondered, *Why two?* But I was about to find out! The red caps had a white "A" on the brim, for All Sport, and so did the warm-up jackets. Black pants, white polo shirts, and cleats completed the outfits, along with clipboards and whistles.

I dressed in the locker room, leaving my costume change and own clothes in the locker marked "Coach." Suddenly, a sensation came over me, one that long since been dormant. It was unmistakable—pre-game jitters. How was I going to do?

The wind was blowing as I walked onto the artificial turf. Cindy pointed out a young guy in a down parka holding a bullhorn.

"Check in with Jamie; he's your director. I'll catch up with you later."

"George, we'll be shooting over there." Jamie pointed to the bench on the fifty-yard line. The rest of the cast was gathering. My two buddies from the audition joined seven other equally large guys all in uniform. Among them was an active New York Giant defensive end and several retired NFL veterans.

I joined the uniformed cast members milling around the fifty-yard line, tossing a football back and forth and chatting. They were a friendly, playful bunch. As I approached, one of them threw me a perfect spiral. I caught the football in my hands and threw it back, not so perfectly.

"Not too bad for an old guy," the passer taunted.

"Places!" Jamie bellowed through his bullhorn.

The wind began to pick up. All of a sudden, the glitter of the stadium and the excitement of playing catch with real-live pros wore off, and my nerves kicked back in. The pretty young producer and the equally attractive makeup girl fussed over me. My red cap with the white "A" for All Sport was cocked at just the right angle. The whistle lanyard around my neck was tucked under the collar of my red jacket, and the producer fussed with the collar of my white sport shirt, making sure it wasn't stuffed into the jacket. She told me to hold the clipboard in my left hand and make sure to look up over it and slightly to the left on command. The makeup girl dabbed my face with powder. Similar minor corrections were repeated to the actors posing as football players.

We lined up with me in front, the tallest of the players behind me, and the rest spread on either side according to height. In front of us were three sets of cameras mounted on wheeled platforms, boom mikes, and a number of technicians milling around.

"Places!" We did a walk-through. I remembered to look up and a little to the left, then waited. Then two burly linemen simulated dumping an orange cooler of Gatorade over my head. *Wait a minute*, I thought.

"Places . . . and . . . action!"

"Hey, Red, are you ready?" From behind me came the voice of one of my friendly tormentors.

The mystery of why two sets of everything was solved abruptly. The shoot was a reenactment of the familiar ritual—the winning couch doused with Gatorade from a large orange vat by two burly linemen. Suddenly the sticky goo washed over my head and cascaded down my neck, trickling down my back under my shirt, settling in my nether region. Even my shoes and socks were saturated. I made squishy sounds when I moved. To make matters worse, after each dousing my "buddies" slapped and patted me on the back to make sure my discomfort was complete, laughing between takes.

"Take two."

"Take three."

The routine was the same. More dousing, more syrupy, stick-to-the-underpants discomfort. Eleven takes in all. By now the novelty had worn off, but the kidding had not.

"Let's give it a rest," Jamie, the director, finally took mercy on me. "Red, why don't you change into the other uniform, the rest can grab a cup of coffee."

We'd been at it for almost three hours.

All I wanted was a hot shower and some dry clothes. My cap was so saturated that orange liquid dribbled from the bill. My hair was beginning to mat. Unfortunately, the water in the locker room had been turned off for the winter. What little heat existed was supplied by several portable electric radiators. I peeled off the first set of clothing, toweled-off, and donned the second outfit. It was dry and felt good.

"Places, places, everyone. This won't take as long!" yelled Jamie.

Four more takes and the shoot was a rap. The drizzle had turned to rain. The wind had picked up again. I was a mess. The director and the cute producer thanked everyone, and the crowd began to dwindle. One of my pals from the audition hollered, "Hey, Red, get your gear. You're coming with us." I grabbed my clothes and packed the first uniform into the duffle bag I had carried from home. A limo driver had pulled up next to the east field gate. My buddies were already seated inside. I opened the door, and one of them handed me an ice-cold Beck's. After the first sip, all of the dousing became a memory. We made a stop on the way to Penn Station at one of their favorite uptown watering holes. One Beck's followed another.

I called Dorothy and asked her to pick me up in Babylon, our local train station. I said my goodbyes and exchanged phone numbers. The limo driver drove me to the railroad station—I was still sticking to the seat—and dumped me there unceremoniously. It was back to reality!

Dorothy was right on time. She made me sit in the backseat on the newspaper she had been reading. Still, stardom had some rewards. I made $200 for the shoot and a memory I'll pass along to my grandchildren. The All Sports drink ad ran in the August addition of *Sports Illustrated*. I bought twenty copies!

My next venture was a part in an ESPN promotion for March Madness, the year-end college basketball tournament, featuring the legendary announcer, Dick Vitale. The commercial featured a number of fans from different walks of life and a number who were just plain different, each one acting out scenes that highlighted different ways of rooting for their teams. One had spiked hair, one had purple hair, one was dressed as a suburban housewife, and another as a distinguished-looking gray-haired banker type in a dark gray business suit. I played the part of an obsessed fan.

The shoot took place in a high school gym in Queens in front of a live crowd with the network sponsors looking on. My call came. My hands were sweaty.

"Action. Take one."

I trotted onto the darkened floor alongside the stands behind the basket. The fans were roaring. A single spotlight followed me. I crouched, arms extended, eyes bulging, and thrust out my hands to catch an imaginary ball, hollering "Give me the rock!" I trotted out of the spotlight to more cheers. Could Hollywood be far off?

The producers were to comb through all of the video clips taken that day and chose several to appear in the final ad. That night I got the call from my agent. I was one of the ones chosen.

Two weeks after the shoot, the phone rang around 11:00 p.m. It was our son Graham from Minneapolis. He and some of his buddies had stopped off at a sports bar after work for a drink.

"Dad, I think I just saw you on TV. What's going on back there?"

The commercial had begun to run. Two days later, Graham's friend Allie called his parents from Sydney, Australia, again from a sports bar. He was in Australia helping prepare Patrick McEnroe for the Australian Open Tennis Championships. "Dad, I could swear I saw George Rider on a TV commercial, please check it out."

I was getting closer to the big time!

There was another call, this time from a different agent. "George, this is Peter. Can you make a 10:30 a.m. call tomorrow?"

"You bet. Thanks."

"You'll be auditioning for the part of a politician giving a speech. Wear or bring a dark suit, shirt, and tie."

The next day I reported to a studio on Tenth Avenue. I was slated and photographed. The whole audition took less than ten minutes. Later that night, the phone rang. "You got the part," Peter said and gave me directions to a studio in Queens. The shoot was scheduled for Friday. I would be part of a music video with Joan Osborne for MTV. I was on a roll. "A musical?" I asked the agent. "I can't sing."

"No, George, a music video. Ask your kids to explain."

I arrived early and was directed to a series of small signs marked Talent. I stood for a moment staring at the signs and savoring them. Then I was directed to Wardrobe, where the wardrobe guy made sure I had no wrinkles. Next it was on to makeup. I was dusted with powder and directed downstairs to the empty set in the center an elevated podium, flanked by a number of American flags on either side. I was thinking about what came next. Then I heard a voice from behind me.

"Hi, George. I'm Joan Osborne. Don't be nervous. You'll do fine. You're great for the part." I turned to greet this attractive and gracious young lady.

She continued, "Don't worry about a thing. Just listen to me." *My pleasure*, I thought. She continued, "The song is called 'St. Teresa.' When the music starts, you'll be at the podium addressing a large crowd. When you hear the words, 'Tell me, tell me,' I'll snap my fingers. Then you start gesturing to the crowd. Point with your arms outstretched. Snap your wrists and point your index fingers. Try it. Be animated. Do it like you mean it!"

Her instructions were perfect. We did it on the first take, which is a director's dream. Joanie (as I now called her) congratulated me and disappeared. I changed clothes. On the way out, I asked one of the technicians where Joanie was. I wanted to say goodbye. I was told that she was busy shooting another scene. He pointed to another set. I walked over. There she was, stretched out in bed with a detached-looking guy. It crossed my mind that I had auditioned for the wrong part. They provided a limo for my ride home. The baby steps toward stardom did not go unnoticed. Dorothy commented jokingly that I was becoming temperamental and difficult to live with!

My last venture was a commercial for Pepsi-Cola. The shoot took place in Elizabeth, New Jersey. I auditioned for the role at a West Side studio in New York, on Twenty-First Street between Sixth and Seventh Avenues. The part was for a bartender. There was the usual slating and pictures, but this time I was asked to stick around. They were one male short for the dance sequence audition. I was paired with an exquisite Russian woman, who was a former ballerina.

The phone rang that night. It was Suzy, my agent. "Congratulations, George. You got the part. You'll get the instructions later. Oh, by the way, they want you for the dancer part, not the bartender." As if on cue, pain radiated through my lower back and legs. I was two months short of a hip replacement. The more I exercised, the more intense it became. The audition had taken place in a small studio. Two turns and a fast click, click, and I was in agony. Do I tell them or suck it up and accept the part? To hell with it! I decided to give it a go.

The day of the shoot, I joined one of the female dancers and several hung-over band members at the Meridian Hotel in Manhattan for an 8:00 a.m. bus trip to the Elks Lodge in Elizabeth, New Jersey. Apparently the Russian ballerina hadn't made the cut.

There were more wardrobe fittings and a longer session in makeup, but I didn't mind.

The choreographer, Natasha, who was on loan from the Arthur Murray Studio in New York, assembled the cast in the downstairs cafeteria for a walk-through after matching up the couples by height. We were going to polka. Panic set in.

"Places, everyone, places. Any questions?"

This was my last chance. The dull pain had started. I had only danced the polka twice in my life, once at a wedding after too many schnapps and once in Halifax at a reception thrown for our destroyer crew on a visit after a naval exercise. I was about to make an ass of myself. I raised my hand. "Natasha, can I have a word with you?" I couched my confession. "I'm a little rusty."

Without hesitation she told the rest of the cast to take a coffee break. She led me to the furnace room, with a cassette player in hand, and gave me a fast tutorial. Ten minutes later we emerged. I had mastered the basic steps. I neglected to mention my bum hip.

We walked through the dance sequence. My partner was a scowling, know-it-all Syd Charisse wannabe. Her whole life was weekend dance competitions. Her best dance was the polka. I didn't stand a chance.

"Got it? Now we'll try it with the music." Natasha turned the cassette on. Suddenly we were twirling to the music in a large circle moving clockwise, all the while Natasha coaching and making suggestions. We finished and rested. My partner never shut up. She liked me about as much as I liked her.

A bell rang. Over the loud speaker we heard, "Cast call."

We all moved up the stairs to the main meeting room, now empty for the shoot, except for a few chairs around the outside. The pain in my hip was still there, dull and throbbing.

This was no fly-by-night production. The director, a large guy with a big smile, was flown in from Hollywood. The polka band was flown in from Chicago and had been featured in the movie *Home Alone.*

The director was standing in front of a mike at the far end of the room, surrounded by the band. The stage was decorated with bright, multicolored bunting. As the band warmed up, he grabbed the mike and gave us more instructions.

I was sitting as far away from little-miss-know-it-all as I could get.

We approached each other on command. The cameras started to roll; the boom mikes were in place.

"Action!"

As the band began to play, a thought crossed my mind: *George, what the hell are you doing here?* I could hardly walk, and I didn't even know how to do the damned dance. My partner wanted to lead. There was no air conditioning. My right knee and ankle were beginning to swell. Pain was beginning to radiate to my left hip, and I was sweating like a pig.

Take one took about four minutes. Once I got going, the pain eased a little, as I focused all my attention on twirling. There would be twenty-two more takes.

I began to improvise to ease the pressure. I spun little-miss-know-it-all out and around, in my best jitterbug move.

"Stop that. That's not how you polka," my partner growled and stepped down hard on my toes.

"Shhhh, I'm leading," and so it went.

Finally, the director shouted, "That's it. It's a wrap."

Before we parted, I tried to ground the heel of my right shoe into my partner's left ankle, but missed. She left without saying a word.

Ten days later, the Pepsi polka commercial began to run nationally. The first time I saw it, I jumped up and pumped my fist in the air. As I landed on my left leg, the pain shot through my hip. Of the five couples, we were the most photographed. A close-up of my spin move was featured twice. I may not be Nureyev, but she was no Syd Charisse either. The pain shot through my body again. The time had come to address my hip problem, and the fact that—despite my beginner's luck—showbiz might be too much of an exacting calling for me after all!

If At First, You Don't Succeed . . .

My ill-fated real estate venture, which ended after prostate surgery, and my recently abandoned acting career due to my bum hip left a huge void in my life. Once again, I was plunked in front of the TV, remote in hand, potato chips in reach, and wife, pets, and kids glaring at me to get a life.

One evening, while I was thumbing through my collection of old *Life* magazines, I rediscovered a story about one of my favorite athletes, Big Daddy Lipscombe, the legendary Baltimore Colts defensive lineman.

The *Life* reporter had asked him, "What makes you so different?"

Big Daddy responded, "When I'm looking to make a tackle, I just keep peeling them off till I find the one with the ball."

Lipscombe's answer defined my efforts to find things I liked to do after retiring.

Enter my daughter Jenny and a great friend of mine named Nat Reed. Nat and I had gone to high school and college together. Nat had been president of our class at Andover and remained very active in alumni activities.

"How would you like to help me out?" he asked me over the phone one night. This was one of his dirty tricks. No one could ever say no to Nat.

"Sure, what would you like?" I replied.

"I'd like you to take over as class secretary."

"What? There must be a bad connection. I thought I heard you say class secretary."

"You did."

"Are you kidding? I can hardly string a sentence together. You can't be serious."

"I certainly am. Three times a year you'll have to write a column for the alumni magazine. I think it's seven hundred words. You'll do fine. I knew I could count on you. The school will be in touch. I'm just a phone call away. There's someone at the door." Click.

I had always liked English as a subject in school, but never sat still long enough to appreciate the finer points, like writing, reading for fun, or just the use and choice of words. I would rush through my assignments and then head outside immediately to the nearest football field or hockey rink.

Could I possibly write a column for the widely read alumni magazine? Did I have a choice? In a foul mood, I called Jenny, who somehow found the whole thing hysterically funny.

Jenny became my editor, typist, researcher, and occasional censor. She came by her skills naturally. She was Phi Beta Kappa at Trinity College in Hartford, Connecticut, and received five English awards at graduation. A play Jenny wrote was included in an anthology put together by Edward Albee of *Who's Afraid of Virginia Woolf* fame. After college, she became a journalist and then a political and corporate speechwriter.

In April 2004, Jenny dragged me kicking and screaming from my perch in front of the TV to my desk. She stood over me until I completed an application to the Southampton Writers Conference, to which she had also applied. We were both accepted, and the conference was to become a yearly event for us.

Interacting with the likes of Pulitzer Prize-winning writers Frank McCourt and Marsha Norman; *Time* magazine columnist Roger Rosenblatt; poet laureate Billy Collins; literary legends Tom Wolfe, Joyce Carol Oates, E. L. Doctorow, and Amy Tan; acting great Alan Alda; and young literary stars Melissa Banks and Matt Klam gave me insights into a world I knew existed, but was never interested enough (or confident enough) to explore.

The first summer, I took a class called "Essays with Roger Rosenblatt." It was the first time I had been in a classroom in fifty years. This time around, I actually paid attention. I arrived early each day, sat up front, and stuffed myself into a desk built for a ninth-grader. Roger was a brilliant teacher. I loved every second of it.

My experience the following year was just as amazing. I signed up for a memoir-writing class with Frank McCourt. Fifteen of us arrived early for the first of five unforgettable sessions, which would be better characterized as productions. Frank was already in the classroom, scribbling on the blackboard and paying no attention to the nervous group of students beginning to take their seats in the shrunken desks behind him. He was sporting a pea-green sports shirt, white pants, and a white hat designed to protect him from the sun.

Suddenly he turned and took a moment to scan the room. You could have heard a pin drop. He announced with an enthusiastic burst of pride, "It's a great day for the Irish! Padraig Harrington has just won the British Open."

Frank went out to spin stories about Limerick, the many hardships he experienced in his childhood, his mother, his brothers, "The English," famous Irish writers, contemporary life, the futility of modern politics, his teaching experiences, the human race, and more—all laced with irreverent invective and usually punctuated with a pixyish grin to make a point. My head was spinning. I was entranced.

Halfway through the second session, it dawned on me that the stories and the way he told them where far from random. Each was illustrative of a point he was making about writing a memoir and wringing out your deepest feelings. Once

I got the hang of it, the total experience sank in and had a profound effect on my determination to get better and carry on with my newfound pleasure.

Frank was generous with his time and individual critiques. His notes on my writing were and are a treasure. He gave me an A (something I rarely if ever achieved in my formal education) with the following comment: "Good George— Lively, Cheeky, Original! Your writing is so youthful, it makes me wonder if you're 23."

Some people are faster learners than others. In my case, it took a half-century to find my true calling. I now get up every morning at 6:00 a.m. and start typing. I usually write for at least five hours a day. My marathon TV sessions are over; I'm far too busy with my newfound pursuit. (I'm still, however, working on weaning myself off the potato chips.)

To date, I have written fifty-plus columns for the alumni magazine. I've also been published multiple times, in literary reviews and newspapers. I started a blog called "Red Rider's Ramblings: Rants, Reminiscences, and Repartee." And I've had the great fortune to find a wonderful agent Anna Termine and publisher, Skyhorse.

Finding your passion after you retire is no easy task. It takes time, patience, and a lot of trial and error. But once you hook onto something you really love doing, you'll find new stores of energy and enthusiasm you never thought you'd have again. You *can* feel younger, happier, and more fulfilled at sixty, seventy, or eighty than you ever did when you were young. Take it from me. Now, excuse me, I have to get back to my writing.

Chapter 3

Where Angels Fear to Tread—The Aches and Pains of Aging

At age eighty-two, getting up each morning is an adventure. I'm not complaining. At least I'm getting up, but the number of aches and pains and the sites where they surface keep increasing with time. (As anyone with roguish proclivities can attest, living life at full throttle can often lead to mishaps and various kinds of boo-boos and ill-begotten injuries!) Whenever I'm feeling achy (which is often), I try to take a few moments to remember the stories behind the shooting pains. They may not make my knees or hips or ankles feel any better, but at least the memories give me a good laugh.

Youthful Indiscretions and Emergency Room Visits

By the time I was a sophomore at Andover, I had logged a lot of time at the infirmary, which was tended by Dr. Roswell Gallagher, the head doctor and a top pediatrician. He was part psychologist, part pill dispenser, and part father figure.

In the course of a few months, I suffered two concussions, one from hockey and one from a well-aimed snowball with a rock in it; a separated left elbow from football; a severed tendon in my right thumb from shattering a milk bottle filled with water; plus stomach and head cold ailments too numerous to mention.

In a letter to my housemaster, Dr. Gallagher characterized these travails as such: "George rushes in where angels fear to tread."

My housemaster then quoted Dr. Gallagher's comments in his term-end report to my parents, in which he presented a rather grim picture.

The following weekend, my parents appeared on campus for meetings with the headmaster, school administrators, my housemaster, teachers, and me. Responsibility was to become the order of the day for me, or else!

The only other medical incident I suffered for the rest of my time at Andover was some torn cartilage, resulting from a clip in the Tufts Freshman football game. I graduated from Andover more or less in one piece and arrived in New Haven, Connecticut, the fall of 1951 to begin my freshman year at Yale.

Not long after that, I had yet another medical mishap from playing lacrosse. The injury, plus the treatment—which involved numerous injections of an anti-coagulant painfully administered in the area just above the knee and extending to my hip-bone—had hobbled me and forced me to use a cane.

One spring day during my freshman year, I was headed back to my room on campus when I noticed that a huge crowd had gathered in the park on the east side of the gated quadrangle.

One group had entrapped Mayor Celentano in the revolving door of the Taft Hotel as a prank. Several undergraduates had jammed the door with tapered wooden pegs to up the ante. His Honor was a little late for lunch.

Another part of the crowd was witnessing democracy in action. Humpty-Dumpty's ice cream truck had dominated a particular corner of the park for a while, but that morning the Good Humor truck arrived first, and a shouting match ensued between the two drivers. What better time and place to debate the "Evils of Big Business." The confrontation drew hordes of students. The rhetoric grew heated and was accompanied by pushing and shoving. Yale law school students were seen taking notes!

New Haven's finest arrived in no mood for niceties on the hot May afternoon. They dispersed the crowd with occasional thrusts of their billy clubs.

I had involuntarily become involved in this fray as I attempted to hobble back to my room with my bum leg and cane.

Fearing for my leg, I tried to stay on the outer edge of the crowd. A wedge of policemen, some on horseback, separated the masses and drove half into the park and the other half toward the one open gate to the freshman campus. Since the gate was small, there was soon a pile-up of students trying to get through. Suddenly, I had no place to go as the police started flailing away with their night sticks. When I was struck by a club on my thigh, I decked the cop who'd hit me.

I woke up on the grass inside the gate. A second policeman had hit me with a blackjack and knocked me out. The police and my classmates then played tug-of-war with my body. Fortunately, Yale won!

I spent several nights in the infirmary. Mother had heard on the morning news all about what was called the "Ice Cream Riot." Five students had been hospitalized. She immediately assumed the worst and called to see if I was a patient. The nurse handed me the phone. My head ached. Mother arrived unannounced the next day to check on me.

Life magazine featured the riot in the next issue, highlighting the struggle between the "evil corporation" and the smaller competitor. My involvement was less about idealism and more about being in the wrong place at the wrong time—and not being able to control my temper. Two major contributing factors to most of the injuries I've sustained throughout my life!

Injured Nowhere Near the Line of Duty

Following college graduation, my injury-prone existence continued when I became an ensign aboard a destroyer homeported in Newport, Rhode Island. On November 6, 1956, we set out from Newport for a deployment with the 6th Fleet in the Mediterranean. On the way over, Gamal Abdel Nasser, the second president of Egypt, blew up several ships, thereby blockading the Suez Canal. We steamed directly to the eastern Mediterranean and patrolled for thirty-one days with our sister ship, the USS *Hale*, and two British destroyers.

We then proceeded to Naples for replenishment and some R&R. A chance meeting with a Yale roommate named John Andrews and a hastily arranged skiing trip to Davos, Switzerland, proved to be my next calamity. This was to be my baptism on skis. I should have known better. John, my instructor, was a Texan.

John convinced me that I really didn't need lessons. We rented skis and boots and boarded the tram to the top of the Parsenn. On the trip up, we engaged two pink-cheeked

British gals in polite conversation. Prior to my first-ever descent, we treated the lasses to a round of Beck's. First mistake. The plot thickened. I tightened my bindings before sliding about three hundred yards into a swarm of kids learning how to ski. Second mistake. I tried to turn, skidded, and fell, catching the tip of my right ski in the snow. I wound up on my bottom, with the right ski tip pointing straight down, and my foot still in the binding. The ski patrol arrived quickly and immobilized my leg, gave me a shot of morphine and a swig of brandy, strapped me to a toboggan, and bounced me down the mountain.

Krankenhaus, Davos, was a busy place, so busy that my ankle was set without the benefit of anesthesia. Instead, I was given morphine and pills and a harmonica-size hard rubber piece to bite, as the doctors tried three times to reset my ankle in the tibia notch and then stuffed my leg in a cast, leaving me weak and hurting.

My roommate (also a catastrophically bad skier) was put in traction and had a pin inserted in his ankle without anesthesia. Sleep that early evening was interrupted by an "angel" pushing a wine cart. We promptly waved her down and put in a huge order.

A few days later, my friend John left to report back to duty. My ship had sailed, and I had to stay put and recuperate hundreds of miles away.

Luckily, our lady skiing friends were attentive, and when I exited the hospital five days later, they helped me find lodging in Davos, where I spent a week, pondering my next steps. My parents were unaware of my predicament (I was afraid to call them). But I was running low on cash. What to do?

I finally picked up the phone and called home.

Mother answered. "Where are you? And why haven't you written?"

"I'm in Davos, Switzerland."

"Where? This is a bad connection—did you say Switzerland? *What* did you break?"

Dad wired me some money the next day. I wrote them a long letter that night and wired the naval dispensary in Naples with my return date.

The doctors in Naples immediately had me flown to the Army's 98th General Field Hospital in Neubrücke, Germany, thirty miles outside Frankfurt. There they wasted no time X-raying my ankle. I was prepped that night and an unsuccessful operation was performed the next day.

Five weeks later, they operated on me again. This time the joint was secured with a pin through my ankle and a full leg cast. As I was being transported back to my room, I saw a comely German nurse and shouted, "Cummen ze here mit da hozen in da hand!" in my sedated state. What I had meant to say was, "Cummen ze here mit da hands a-hoven! ("Surrender! Come here with your hands up!"). Instead, what had come out was, "Come here with your pants in your hand!"

That story soon made the rounds. After the operation, I had another problem—I hadn't been able to take a pee. The nurses tried everything, but as a last resort, they showed me a large catheter and a syringe and said that if I didn't produce, they would insert it in the proper place.

I blurted out, "For Christ's sake! That thing is bigger around than what I've got!" I immediately began peeing all over my bed and became a staff favorite overnight.

The rehab was grueling. I was shocked when the full leg cast was finally replaced with a walking cast. I looked at my leg. It resembled an ugly swizzle stick.

My roommate by now was another Navy officer. Ed hurt himself trying to impress a lady friend at the officers club in Banoli, Naples, by doing chin-ups. He had jumped to grab a tree limb, unaware of the ten-foot drop to the street below. The limb had snapped, and he fell, crushing his elbow and wrist. Ed's surgery took place between my two operations. Ed also became a hospital "favorite."

There were seventy nurses on staff. As our mobility returned, Ed and I frequented the officers' club, along with this flock of Florence Nightingales. The club was an unpretentious one-story brick building with a bar, piano, card tables, a dart board, and a jukebox. Our only competition for the ladies in white was a handful of older single officers, dull from age and long deployments. It was like pheasant hunting with an elephant gun!

Ed left in April. I left two weeks later. The night before my departure, the staff gave me a going away party.

Early the next morning, orderlies entered my room with a stretcher.

While in Europe, I had purchased items for my family. There were perfume and linen tablecloths for Mom, a special electric shaver for Gramp, beer steins for my brother Ken, and three bottles of vintage brandy for Dad. When the orderlies left the room, I lined up the three bottles of brandy between my legs on the stretcher under the blanket, and then waited for the orderlies to carry me to the bus.

The trip to the airport took about an hour. We were loaded one by one onto the four-engine military transport plane. The stretchers were secured in place, three deep on either side of the aisle.

I was the middle of three stretchers. Two lung patients were located forward, just aft of the bulkhead that separated the cockpit from the cabin. Twenty minutes into the flight, the cabin pressure dropped sharply. The lung patients' breathing became labored. The pilot put the plane into a steep dive to adjust the pressure. The bottles between my legs piled up in a very tender spot. It was like taking a Messier slap shot in the groin with no tinny. We circled once and landed.

A second plane was waiting for us. An hour into the flight, I looked out at the right wing. The inboard propeller slowed and then stopped. I pulled at a flight nurse's arm as she walked down the aisle. "The . . . the . . . the . . . engine just stopped," I told her. The guy on the stretcher directly across from me hollered, "Hey, nurse, one of the engines over here just quit, too." Any lingering discomfort I had from playing backstop for the brandy bottles disappeared.

The pilot headed back, and the return flight was nerve-racking. When the plane touched down, we gave the pilot a lying down ovation. Four of us were billeted in a building for the night, and we wasted no time hobbling down to the officers' club in our pajamas. Smoke hung heavily in the air and the decibel level was high. A waiter took our order, and the adventures of the day began to fade. A tall, gray-haired colonel ambled over and ordered drinks all around. Seated at his table were six officers, including the pilot and co-pilot of our second flight. They made room for us at their table and there we spent a very enjoyable evening.

The following afternoon, we were trussed up again for the third time in two days. We were headed for Gander, Newfoundland. Two and a half hours into the flight, the intercom crackled, "We're having a bit of a problem with the automatic pilot and will be turning to spend the night at Lajes, in the Azores." I was beginning to feel jinxed.

The flight resumed early the next day. We refueled at Gander and set down at our destination, McGuire Air Force Base in New Jersey, more than fifty hours after our estimated time of arrival.

My parents went through a nasty ordeal trying to get details about what was causing the flight delays, and when I would actually arrive. As the plane made its final approach, fire trucks and ambulances raced to the far end of the runway. This was a normal precaution unfamiliar to my mother, and it unnerved her even more.

At long last, my stretcher was finally placed on the ground. I spotted Dad, grabbed the three brandy bottles (one now almost empty), and hobbled toward him as fast as I could. Mom was right behind him. I was reminded once again how fortunate I was to have such loving parents.

If anything can be learned from my escapades, it is this: Your body *is* your temple, and you should treat it as such. It's also never too late to get religion when it comes to caring for your health.

In recent years, I have added one new hip and removed one bum prostate. I've tried to keep in shape by walking in the local YMCA pool four times a week and lifting weights. So far I'm still mobile, and I'm fighting every day to stay that way.

It took decades of being a hell-raiser for me to finally learn my lesson. I no longer rush in where angels fear to tread. I dip my toe in first, and then wade around awhile before I take the plunge. It took me three-quarters of a century and multiple surgeries to figure that out, but that's the thing about getting older—it makes you wiser, whether you want to be or not!

Chapter 4

Get a Job, Who Me?
Teaching Grandkids
Responsibility

My eldest grandson turned fifteen this past June. His birthday prompted a discussion about his plans for the summer. He spent the past two summers recovering from extensive orthopedic surgeries to correct a growth disorder in his arms and legs. For the first time since he became a teenager, he was ready, willing, and able to get his first real summer job. He couldn't wait.

I sat him down and gave him one of my stern grandfatherly lectures. "Getting a job is no easy task, young man,"

I chided. "It takes focus and discipline, along with a stellar work ethic. You need to show them you are a leader—that you're the type of person who will always go the extra mile. You have to be hungry and make a first impression they'll never forget."

I was on a roll . . . and then I put my glasses on and looked over at my grandson.

What I didn't realize was that the whole time I'd been talking to him, he'd been fidgeting on his iPhone or iPad or iSomething or other.

"Did you hear anything I just said?" I waved my finger at him.

"Sure, Poppy, you said getting a job is hard. And I'm sure what you're about to say—because you always say the same thing—is that things were a heck of lot harder when you were my age, right?"

I paused. He was impertinent, absolutely. But, he was also spot-on, as usual. I wasn't sure whether to scold him for being fresh or pat myself on the back for producing such an intelligent little son-of-a-gun.

"Correct," I informed him. "You have no idea how tough it was . . ." I was just about to launch into the story, when his phone began to chirp. "Sorry, Poppy. Dad says I have to go home and study for my math test." (I'm sure my son and grandson were somehow in cahoots.)

"Okay, Ace," I gave him a hug. "I'll write the story down for you." Off he went. I poured myself a new cup of coffee and sat at the computer and began to type.

Time: the late 1950s. Public school, boarding school, college, the Navy Reserves Officers' Training Corps, then sea duty on the destroyers USS *Preston* and USS *Abbot*. So far my maturing process had been full and routine, but I had not yet pushed the get-serious button.

My failed attempt at becoming the next Jean-Claude Killy, the fabled French Olympic skier, had left me with an atrophied right leg, a pin in my right ankle, a broken fibula, a pair of aluminum arm crutches, and way too much time on my hands.

Had it not been for my self-imposed hiatus, I might well have made the Navy my career. I had taken to my duties enthusiastically. I was a fast learner and loved the new challenges. The captain took particular interest in me and spent extra time teaching me the intricacies of navigation and ship handling, allowing me to practice while learning. He wrote a letter of recommendation for me when I first started looking for a job that I cherish to this day.

Fast-forward five months. I was now at home recuperating at the family beach cottage in Lonelyville, Fire Island. Mom was the chief cook and bottle washer. The three of us—Mother, our faithful lab Sam, and I—spent the first few weeks of the summer sunning, eating, and catching up.

Dad, Gramp, and my step-grandmother Ruth joined us every weekend.

I had loved every minute of my Navy service and spent a great deal of my time kicking myself for being so stupid. I really missed the ship and my shipmates, as well as my brother Ken, who was still aboard.

On my second bi-monthly checkup at St. Albans Naval Hospital, the short leg cast was removed. The sight of my skinny, hairy twig of a leg made me even madder at myself. I pursued my rehab with a vengeance, doing prescribed exercises, swimming, and walking, tentatively at first. My rediscovered mobility and night-time forays convinced me to start giving swimming lessons.

I still had eight more weeks to go before the scheduled removal of the pin in my ankle, and I had to do something to keep busy and make enough spending money to fund my evening exploits.

My swim "school" began to catch on. One of the mothers, a divorced French countess, caught my eye and soon became more than a passing fancy. Charleen was five years my senior, with a six-year-old son in tow. (Note to grandson: this in no way condones you dating a French countess "cougar" when you get older.)

When it was time for Charleen to meet my mother, we planned late afternoon cocktails on our deck. To say that I was a little nervous would be an understatement. Mom made deviled clams. There was vodka for Charleen. Everything was set. I had not thoroughly briefed Mother. Some details had been left out.

Charleen arrived at the stroke of five. Alas, I had neglected to tell Mother about Jason, the six-year-old trailing along behind her. I had also left out the fact that Charleen was divorced and several years my senior. The conversation was awkward, but cordial. After one drink, Charleen and Jason departed. I would join them later, but not before a thorough grilling by an inquisitive and underinformed mother.

"George, what a nice girl!" my mother exclaimed. "You never mentioned anything about her son. Where do they live in the winter? Jason will probably be going to school soon. How old did you say she was?"

Her questions were asked in such a way that answering them made me focus on more than Charleen's striking beauty, her come-hither curves, and her endless appetites. (Note to grandson: that's "appetite" in terms of food, of course.)

It was obvious that Mother was sure that I was getting in over my head. I sidestepped the barrage, making repeated trips to the kitchen to clear the glasses and plates from the deck. I thanked Mother and excused myself, mumbling that I was late for picking up the babysitter. Charleen and I had plans for dinner.

Charleen traveled in high circles and offered to make introductions for me to some of her successful business friends, if I ever decided to look for a real job. (A what?) Somewhere on the periphery of my radarscope a faint blip had disturbingly appeared. The world of shoes and suits was rapidly approaching.

I began to dread weekend dinners with my family. Innocent questions asked in an offhand manner with an increasingly similar theme were lobbed at me.

"George, you have your choice—rare or medium on the steak. By the way, have you talked to John Phillips lately? How does he like First Boston?" This was Dad's typical low-key approach.

Gramp would chime in, "George, please pass the salt. Have you changed your mind on becoming a doctor? Have you given any thought to banking? Your Yale economics degree would come in handy."

The drumbeat continued. The final straw occurred at swimming lessons one late August afternoon. Jason told me that he would be a first-grader in September. He then looked at me and asked, "What are *you* going to do when you go home this fall?"

Charleen again offered to set up a meeting with one of her well-positioned friends. This time I paid attention. She arranged for me to meet a man named Peter Grace for lunch at the City Midday Club. Peter was part of the Grace Steamship family and also a top Wall Street financier and banker.

The one suit I owned was steaming around the Atlantic in my brother's stateroom locker. I ad-libbed an outfit to wear to the lunch that consisted of a white shirt and regimental tie borrowed from Dad, a pair of worn chinos, a navy blue blazer that had seen better days, and a pair of old loafers, rounded at the heels, with no socks.

Not only was I overmatched sartorially—everyone else in the club was dressed to the nines—but much of the Q&A at lunch went right over my head. I was ill at ease from the start. Peter was very nice. I knew when we shook hands and said goodbye that I had totally underwhelmed him. Thank the Lord and Charleen for that lunch. It was clear how much I had to learn about so many things. I wasn't even a diamond in the rough.

I returned to the beach chastened and a bit downcast. Charleen and I enjoyed the last days of summer. There were no more swim lessons, but still plenty of time for the ocean and dinners out or cooked in. She and Jason left on Labor Day.

The procedure to remove the pin from my ankle was scheduled for the first week in September at St. Albans Naval Hospital. Charleen had a surprise for me: tickets for the semi-final U.S. Tennis Championship matches at Forrest Hills. We arranged to meet for brunch at a trendy little restaurant she had chosen.

We walked to the stadium after the brunch. On the way to her box, she introduced me to Pat and Dick Nixon. The weather was great; the tennis even better. We left at four o'clock. Her limousine driver knew all the shortcuts to St. Albans. We arrived early for my check-up. After tests and prepping, the operation was scheduled for two days later. Charleen walked me to the door of the hospital. We kissed.

"George! I don't want to go back to the social scene. I don't want to go back to Europe. I don't want you ever to have to wear a suit. Why can't we just go back to the beach and stay forever? You should be free to roam the dunes and beaches barefoot. Instead you'll get caught up in the rat race that is called living. Don't ever give up your wanderlust and thirst for adventure. Always remember what we had, if it was only for three months." She squeezed my hand and rushed back to the limo. I waved and called out. Something told me that I would never see her again.

The next day, more tests. I missed a call from Charleen. She left a message wishing me luck. My fling with the French countess gradually began to fizzle. The intensity remained, but the future did not.

Mid-morning the following day the pin was removed without incident. Dad picked me up two days later. The surgeon told me I had permanently lost fifteen degrees of motion in my right ankle and that I would suffer from arthritis that could be crippling as I aged. He offered me an immediate medical discharge, but I refused without hesitation. The injury was my fault. I requested return to active duty to finish my duty tour that December. I loved every minute of my service, especially the time spent at sea.

As I prepared for the end of my active duty, I augmented my wardrobe with two new suits, regular shoes, socks, and several snappy ties. One of my college buddies recommended a career planner.

I made an appointment with the planner one late afternoon as my discharge date approached. It cost me a hundred dollars up front. That didn't help my mental state. The world seemed to be closing in on me. The interview was formal, and the questions seemed too intrusive. "Which do you like better, A or B? Where do you want to be when you're thirty, forty, and then fifty?" Then there was the aptitude test. When I checked the results, I was amused to hear that high on my list of suggested vocations was piano manufacturing. The test also established that I had pugilistic tendencies. The thought crossed my mind that the hundred bucks could have bought a lot of beer and a couple of good steak dinners. I never booked a follow-up appointment.

Gramp called me one evening and suggested that I call Landon Thorne, his best friend, to discuss my future. Mr. Thorne was legendary. During and after the Great Depression, his financial expertise helped salvage a number of major eastern utility companies. He also served on the boards of Chubb and Sons, Bankers Trust, Southern Pacific Rail Road, and City Bank (now Citibank), among others.

I'll never forget the meeting at his Wall Street office in the Bankers Trust Building. The suite was like a movie set, with ship models and nautical oil paintings dotting the dark paneled walls, rounded out with an elegant dining room, kitchen, and bar. Mr. Thorne looked like an actor himself. He was a tall, handsome man with an athletic build in a dark blue pinstriped suit.

"George, tell me what you'd like to do," he asked me from the other side of his desk.

"Banking interested me in college. My economics degree should come in handy." We talked for twenty minutes at the end of which he picked up the phone and called a friend, the chairman of City Bank. The arrangements were underway. We shook hands, and I thanked him. The die was cast. As I exited, he said, "Say hello to your grandfather and good luck."

I can't remember if written resumes were required in those days, but I do remember clearly my first encounter with a personnel department. I arrived at City Bank fifteen minutes early, outfitted in a new dark blue suit, shiny black shoes, white button-down shirt, regimental tie, socks, and my equally new dark brown leather briefcase. The assistant personnel director's secretary handed me a stack of forms to fill out. Halfway through the chore, she interrupted me. "Mr. Rider, Mr. Richardson will see you now. You can leave your papers with me and finish them later."

I had three interviews in close succession, each one covering different areas of the bank: domestic banking, international banking, and the trust department. All of these interviews were conducted by senior VPs, who all seemed impressive, knowledgeable, and genuinely interested in what I had to say.

By the end of the day, I had completed the paperwork and was leaning toward International Banking, maybe in South America where I could use my four years of Spanish.

I was asked to report back the next morning at 10:00 a.m. I had an appointment with the head of the personnel department. Again I arrived early and eager. So far, so good! I was now cocky and sure of myself, not a good combination that early in the game. The same receptionist called my name. "Mr. Davis will see you now." Mr. Davis rose from his desk, greeted me, and before we even sat down, he proceeded to tell me that he had heard great things about me from his boss Mr. Moore, who was chairman of the board. Mr. Davis suffered from what my parents called Locust Valley lockjaw, a form of malocclusion adopted by some for effect and an affectation I'd heard at boarding school and college over the years that instantly made my hackles go up. He had obviously read my forms and kept calling me Buddy. At one point he leaned over close to me as if to impart a secret.

"George, you know that we here at City have become very democratic." I listened intently. "We actually hired a Rutgers graduate this year for the training program." I couldn't believe that he was serious. I looked at him and started to laugh, as though I had just heard a joke. The look on his face said it all. I had made a mistake, a very bad mistake.

There was a pause, an awkward silence. He looked down, avoiding eye contact with me and began to shuffle papers on his desk. After what seemed like a lifetime, he thanked me for coming. As I got up to leave, the door opened and in strode Mr. Moore, the chairman, ready to greet the new trainee, recommended by his good friend Landon Thorne. We shook hands.

Mr. Davis was momentarily at a loss for words. He asked me to step outside. Minutes later they joined me. Mr. Davis announced that I would be hearing from them in a few days. The interview was over. Three days later, while staying with my parents, a letter arrived that read: "At this time we are sorry that we cannot offer you a position."

How the hell was I going to tell Gramp and Mr. Thorne?

Gramp dropped by on the weekend. He already knew. He announced that Landon wanted to see me in his office bright and early Monday.

"Listen to what he has to say. You did fine up to a point."

Monday morning I was back in Mr. Thorne's office. This time I felt like I was sitting on a bag of live eels.

"George, don't be too quick to answer questions," he advised. "Think about what you're going to say before you say it. Talk slowly. You will do well. By the way, on your way out, stop at the sixth floor and ask the receptionist for Bill Snow. He's head of personnel at Bankers Trust. He's expecting you."

My only thought upon entering Mr. Snow's office was, *God, George, don't screw up again.*

Mr. Snow and I talked for twenty minutes about the Navy, life in general, banking, and related topics. I handed him my letter of recommendation from W. W. Deventer, Commander U.S. Navy (my former captain), to help bolster my case. In it, Captain Deventer wrote, "I find George Rider to be of very high character, moderate habits, and completely reliable. . . . It is your good fortune that Mr. Rider chose your firm. The Navy regrets his departure and would welcome him back. And I personally would be there to greet him." (I wasn't so sure about "moderate habits," but I was thrilled by the words of praise from a man of such distinction). Mr. Snow nodded as he read it, as though he seemed impressed, and I breathed a brief sigh of relief. But my guard was still up.

"George, I'd like you to have a talk with the head of training, Otis Brown."

"Thank you, Mr. Snow." I was still walking on eggshells.

Mr. Brown was equally nice, but more reserved. "Come in, George, I've heard a lot about you." (I bet he had.) We discussed my interests, and he outlined the training program. We talked about the Navy and my athletic achievements. The time sped by. I had been there for close to an hour. My guard was slipping, without me even knowing it.

"George, I see you majored in economics," Mr. Brown noted, looking at my college transcript.

"Yes, sir."

"What did you think of Econ. 10?"

I blurted out, "Econ. 10 was the worst course I had ever taken. Plodding, ponderous, and pointless. It was a complete waste of time."

A smile spread on Mr. Brown's face. He said, matter-of-factly, "George, before joining Bankers, ten years ago, I taught economics at Yale. I wrote the syllabus for Econ. 10."

My heart sunk. "Oh, shit!" I muttered. "I've done it again." "Calm down, George, you're the first student or ex-student who has ever told me the truth. You'll hear from us shortly." I left, kicking myself. The letter arrived, and I opened it, hands shaking. Not only was I hired, they were going to pay me $95 a week! I found out later that only two of us were paid $95; the rest of the trainees were earning $85 or less.

On my first day at work, I exited the IRT at Broadway by Trinity Church dressed in a new suit and carrying my briefcase. The sun was bright, a stiff northwest breeze was blowing, and the flags on the buildings were flapping from the flagpoles. I crossed Broadway on my way to 16 Wall Street. I had done it. I was going to be a banker!

From behind me I heard, "George, where's your hat?"

I snapped back, "Dad warned me that wearing a hat was a sure way to go bald." There striding up next to me was Mr. Snow—a dead ringer for Yul Brynner.

"George, you're getting better, but you're not quite there yet." (I'm still working on "getting there" more than a half a century later!)

When I finished writing about my first job memories, I took the last sip of my coffee and pressed "print." I re-read the story and decided perhaps this was not quite the right message for my fifteen-year-old grandson, at least not yet. I scribbled at the top of the page: "For Grahamie, when he gets a little older . . . Let's hope you inherit some common sense genes from your grandmother's side of the family!"

Chapter 5

Thanksgiving Day Turkey Shoot—Let's Hear It for Family Holidays!

The older I get, the more I look forward to and cherish family holidays (or at least the warm, fuzzy feeling I get when the day is done, there's been no bloodshed, and the fridge is stuffed with yummy leftovers). There's nothing like waking up in the morning and knowing that my progeny will soon be arriving from near and far—or in my case, from right next door (son, daughter-in-law, and grandkids) and New York City (daughter, son-in-law, and granddog). I leap out of bed (okay, limp is more like it), whip up a hot breakfast and coffee (well, in truth, wait for my beloved to hand me a diet breakfast shake), and reflect on the warm, poignant, gauzy-filtered memories of past holidays spent with family. There's no better way to prepare yourself for the onslaught of kids and grandkids—and the inevitable brawls over who gets the remote control and whether or not I'm allowed a second Scotch—than remembering back to your childhood to what holidays at your house were *really* like.

There is one Thanksgiving I remember very vividly. The year was 1944, and I was twelve years old. In addition to the turkey and stuffing, this particular day also included theft, shotgun blasts, state troopers, and a neighbor bleeding profusely from a self-inflicted razor wound.

The setting: The small town of Brightwaters, Long Island. More specifically, my Aunt T. and Uncle K.'s house.

The cast: In addition to my aunt and uncle, the gathering included Gramp, my revered but distant grandfather, who was the patriarch of the family and a respected doctor, author, and bank president; Ruth, his second wife; and my parents, who for some reason were constantly kicking me outside to play, along with my ten-year-old brother Ken and our younger cousins, Tony and Mike.

The annual routine: The adults would arrive early in the day so that they had ample time to down several rounds of old fashioneds before Gramp arrived. He took a dim view of drinking of any sort, so, to pacify him while making Thanksgiving with the family more palatable, the adults pushed up the start of the cocktail hour. As my British dad used to say, "It's noon somewhere in the Empire."

When the doorbell rang, glasses were hastily secreted under the couch, under a chair, and behind a large framed picture of my aunt in her wedding dress on the piano. Gramp entered, followed by Ruth. Their coats were hung in the vestibule closet. The grandsons were lined up to greet him. Ruth headed straight for the kitchen "to help," muttering hellos on the way. Her first order of business was to retrieve the chilled drink awaiting her in the icebox, compliments of Uncle K.

Mother and Aunt T. soon followed. Back then, they took turns preparing Thanksgiving and Christmas dinners at their neighboring homes in Brightwaters. Because of the war and stretched budgets, the halcyon days of having cooks and maids and elaborate feasts had come to a screeching halt, and the time-honored familial rules of decorum had already begun to fray.

Dad was on his way back to the living room when he happened to open the door to the attached garage out of curiosity. To his surprise and consternation, he spied two incarcerated turkeys quietly contemplating their uncertain future. Uncle K. had received them as a gift from a friend in South Carolina. They were billeted in a cage with a latch that was secured by a large wooden peg.

Action was called for, or so Dad thought. He removed the peg, folded the latch back, and opened the garage door. He returned to the chair he had vacated in the living room just moments before, with no one the wiser. Gramp was clucking over his four grandsons, who were soon ordered outdoors (yet again) to play. Just about this time, the delivery boy from our local ice cream parlor appeared with the dessert.

We kids had just started to play catch in the backyard when Cousin Tony noticed that the garage door was open. He went to check and let out a war whoop. "The turkeys are missing!" Gramp and Uncle K. burst from the house. After each of the grandchildren had sworn we weren't involved in the heist, they concluded immediately that the culprit had to be the delivery boy. Uncle K. placed a call to a buddy of his at the state police barracks.

Dad was trying to be as inconspicuous as possible. He was happy for the turkeys and their newfound freedom, but getting more than a little concerned about the fate of the unsuspecting delivery boy.

"We've got to retrieve the turkeys. Boys, start looking!" Uncle K. commanded.

Meanwhile, in a nearby house, Donny Anderson was shaving. "Uncle" Donny and "Aunt" Bunny (they were close family friends rather than relatives) lived near a wooded lot that had been cleared for a victory garden for the neighborhood.

Uncle Donny had over-imbibed the night before with several of his Wall Street partners. He decided to sleep in and arose near noon to ready himself. Still in his pajamas and all lathered up, Uncle Donny absentmindedly looked out the window. There, perched on the ledge, was a live turkey staring right at him. Startled, his hand jerked, and the straight razor opened a gash in his left cheek.

"Bunny, Bunny! Come quick, there's a turkey staring at me!" he yelled.

Still annoyed by her husband's antics from the night before, Aunt Bunny opened the bathroom door. The turkey had disappeared into the woods, and there stood her husband bleeding profusely from the four-inch slash in his cheek.

"Donny," she screamed at him. "Your drinking is getting out of hand!"

Back at Uncle K.'s and Aunt T.'s, the search for the turkeys continued. A neighbor phoned Uncle K. to tell him that he had seen a live turkey entering another neighbor's barn. Uncle K. calmly unlocked the gun cabinet in the den, took out a sixteen-gauge double-barreled shotgun and four shells, and headed for the neighbor's property with Gramp in close pursuit.

Shortly after they departed, two uniformed troopers appeared at the front door. Brightwaters was and still is a small community. In those days, everyone knew everyone, including the troopers. Dad ushered them into the den where the bar was set up and poured them each a stiff holiday drink. He promptly confessed, "*I* liberated the turkeys," thereby getting the delivery boy off the hook. The troopers, sworn to secrecy, finished their drinks, exited smiling, and returned to their barracks.

Suddenly there was the sound of a shotgun blast. *Bang!* Uncle K. had spotted one of them perched on an overhead platform in the neighbors' barn. He took aim, fired the gun, and the turkey dropped to the garage floor, followed by a haze of feathers fluttering in the light from the new hole that had just appeared in the barn's back wall. Gramp and Uncle K. walked back with what was left of the fugitive fowl. The rest of us continued to look for turkey number two.

When we returned from "the hunt" empty-handed, the doorbell rang again. It was Uncle Donny, still clad in his pajamas, robe, and slippers and sporting an oozing bandage. Bunny followed at a discreet distance. One look at the cut convinced Gramp that further treatment was called for.

"Georgie! Get my bag from the car!" Gramp instructed me. He always traveled with his medicine bag, which included a complete set of surgical instruments and other necessary items for emergency repairs.

Uncle Donny was led to the dining room, which had the best light in the house, and was seated in one of Aunt T.'s antique chairs.

A basin of water was heated on the stove. Ruth and Mother cleared the crystal water glasses, Wedgewood china, and place settings from the near end of the table, and then covered the linen tablecloth with towels from the powder room.

Gramp told Donny to lie down on top of the table and gave him two shots of Novocain. There were eight stitches in all.

Aunt Bunny, still barely speaking to her husband, deferred viewing the repairs in favor of downing a double Scotch in the den as Uncle K. was replacing the sixteen-gauge in the gun cabinet. As Gramp proceeded, the grown-ups disappeared one by one to join Bunny. Those passing in the hall could hear the unmistakable sounds of ice cubes clinking in glasses.

The last stitch in place, Gramp excused himself, moved a strainer full of peas to the side of the kitchen sink, and washed his hands and instruments before returning to the living room to read the paper.

Mother and Ruth removed the water basin, the bloodied monogrammed towels, and the gauze pads and placed them in the kitchen sink, next to the instruments and boiled peas, and just a few inches away from the stove where Thanksgiving dinner was simmering over a low flame. The table was reset.

Uncle Donny stopped by the den to thank Uncle K. and joined Aunt Bunny, who had now mellowed perceptibly. They finally exited after thanking Gramp, and dinner was served two and a half hours later as though nothing had happened.

Just before we sat down at the table, the phone rang. Aunt T. answered. "It's for you, dear. The troopers' barracks."

"Sir, after a lengthy interrogation, we have concluded that the delivery boy did not let the turkeys loose," the trooper informed Uncle K. "We'll continue investigating and keep you informed. Happy Thanksgiving!" Dad greeted the news with a smile and an extra big swig from his glass tumbler.

Two years later, just before dessert was served, Dad clinked his water glass with his butter knife, rose from his chair, and cleared his throat. "I have a confession to make. I let the turkeys go."

Uncle K. was furious; Mother was even madder.

All eyes turned to Gramp. He looked out sternly over his thick glasses, glancing around the table from face to face, and finally fixed his eyes on Dad. He began to laugh. "That was a day for the ages." Dad looked more than a little relieved. Gramp stood up, raised his half-filled water glass, and toasted, "To family." The grown-ups smiled and toasted back, "To family," then one by one disappeared to refill their glasses. Once again, we were told to go out and play.

You may wonder whatever happened to turkey number two. He was cornered and captured the next day. Uncle K. pardoned him, and he lived out his life on their farm on the East End of Long Island. I imagine the little fellow may have had somewhat mixed feelings about joining the clan.

The next time you prepare for a big family gathering, take a few moments to reflect back on family holidays gone by. It will give you a few good belly laughs, remind you that the perfect world of "Ozzie and Harriet" never really existed, and get you ready to embrace another big day of family fun and dys-*fun*-ction!

Chapter 6

11 Maple Avenue: Death of A Landmark

On January 30, 2006, at exactly 9:00 a.m., the past, present, and future collided. I was reviewing notes for a talk I was about to give. A sleet storm from the night before had left puddles that were just beginning to thaw. Early arrivals were chatting, drinking coffee, and munching on buns or bagels under the open-sided tent, which had been set up for the occasion. Several very large trucks were positioned to help cart away the debris from the pending demolition.

A large, motorized crane was noisily maneuvering itself to begin its work. The metal ball suspended from the slightly angled arm would soon pulverize the back wall of 11 Maple Avenue, a beloved three-story building built in 1918.

This was going to be a big day for the community. 11 Maple had fallen into disrepair and become a blight on the landscape, due to a lack of proper oversight by those in authority. Eighty-plus poor souls were forced to live in squalor in the single-room occupancy residence, which had once been a symbol of healing and hope.

In a monumental undertaking, the Chamber of Commerce led by President Donna Perricone spearheaded the relocation of each of these residents, and individuals in the community contributed freely to defray their moving expenses and provide rent security.

But despite this victory, the thought of the events about to transpire had my stomach in a knot. I was already nervous enough about addressing the crowd of citizens, political figures, press, family, and friends who were about to witness the demolition of what was originally Dr. King's Hospital, the first private hospital in Suffolk County, New York. I stood along the sidelines and let my mind travel back in time.

My grandfather, Dr. George S. King, was a towering figure in the town of Bay Shore and all across Suffolk County. He was born in 1878 to Elbert King, a New York City policeman, and his wife Ellen. The King family had first come to this country a generation earlier when my grandfathers' grandfather had stowed away on the *Joseph John Cummings* from Ireland. The ship foundered in a storm off Patchogue, Long Island, and Patrick King came ashore, clinging to a rum keg (or so the story goes). He settled there and began his new life of farming.

Elbert died in his early thirties in 1885, leaving behind a wife and three young children, Alda, Lotta, and George, who moved back to Patchogue. Gramp graduated number one in his high school class at the age of sixteen and entered New York Medical School. (Back in those days, you didn't have to attend college before medical school.) He graduated number one in his class once again and interned on Blackwell's Island (now Roosevelt Island), which was home to the disenfranchised and the poor. Gramp began his practice in Brooklyn, but soon the lure of the Great South Bay, the salt water, and the outdoors drew him to Bay Shore, where he had fished and sailed as a boy. He moved there in 1901.

Bay Shore was a bustling hamlet at the turn of the century that boasted an affluent summer population and a thriving movie industry. Initially, Gramp—a young, hungry, half-Irish farm kid from another town—was shunned and branded as an upstart by the entrenched medical community. He was a Methodist and teamed with Father Donavan, the Roman Catholic priest, to tend to the poor and downtrodden in the area. Soon word of his skill and hard work spread, and his practice began to flourish.

He charged fifty cents for an office visit and a dollar for a house call. Babies were delivered (mostly in the home) for ten bucks. Gramp's concern for those in need never wavered. As his practice grew and the hospital was completed, new office staff learned that Gramp's billing code "C.T.G." meant "Charge to God." He was responsible for the first X-ray machine and the first emergency room in Suffolk County.

My thoughts turned back to the demolition that was about to take place. The wrecking ball was aimed at the emergency room, which had seen so many heartaches and answered prayers. Gramp celebrated fifty years of practice on June 9, 1952, with a party at Southward Ho, the local country club. Now adults, one thousand of the five thousand babies he delivered attended the gala. The *New York Herald Tribune* featured the story and a family portrait on the front page of the Sunday edition. Gramp sold the hospital in 1963 after he retired. He was eighty-five and a local legend.

He found time in his later years to author an autobiography and a sea tale that was made into the movie *The Slave Ship*, starring Wallace Beery and marking the debut of Mickey Rooney as the cabin boy. William Faulkner wrote the screenplay and Darryl Zanuck was the producer. Gramp was also chairman of the First National Bank of Bay Shore and one of its founders.

My reveries were interrupted by the arrival of my lovely daughter-in-law Paulette with her sons Graham Jr. and Bradley in tow. Standing nearby were my wife Dorothy and our daughter Jenny. It was so cold that you could see everyone's breath. The boys were transfixed by the heavy equipment that was about to crush the building that symbolized so much of our family history.

I was a year younger than Graham Jr. when I almost died from what appeared to be appendicitis. I had double pneumonia and, to complicate matters, I shot a temperature of more than 105 degrees. My parents rushed me to Gramp's hospital, and he summoned a team of specialists from New York City, including a brilliant young surgeon from Columbia Presbyterian named Dr. Caldwell B. Esselstyne. After the operation, a state trooper sped to New York to pick up a sample of the new sulfa drug, which was immediately administered. My temperature finally broke, and I spent two weeks in the hospital, most of the time in an oxygen tent.

My ground floor room overlooked Maple Avenue. Mother told me that Dad would come to the hospital every night to sit with me while I slept and assure me, "Everything is going to be okay, my blessed darling." After he left, he would pace by the window until the lights were dimmed.

Donna Perricone interrupted my thoughts. It was time to get ready for my speech, but first several town dignitaries would speak before I did. One told the story of Dr. King's Park, which was dedicated to Gramp in 1965 and is now the home of a beautiful band shell for performances by local musicians. From here, you can see the bulkhead on a creek where Gramp's skiff, *The Ruff "n" Ready*, had been tied up behind his house.

As I was finishing my remarks, I acknowledged the new owner of the property, who planned to turn it into a luxury condo complex, thus completing one of the final stages of redevelopment for our downtown. I concluded by saying, "Today starts a new day for 11 Maple Avenue and a new day for Bay Shore."

I moved away from the podium and looked back at the building, but didn't see much through my tears. The crane operator swung the arm into the back wall. All of a sudden, I felt a little hand gripping mine. I looked down to see my grandson Graham. He said, "Don't be sad, Poppy. Everything's going to be okay."

Gramp had set the bar high for the four generations to follow. But his biggest legacy was his devotion to family. Eleven Maple, a landmark to our clan, may have come down, but the memories, the pride, and the commitment we have to one another still stand, and I pray always will.

It's not easy to see the landmarks of your youth—your childhood home, the park your kids played in, an old church whose congregation has died off—be destroyed or left to slowly decay. But I've found when change comes, you can at least preserve and honor the past by writing down your memories of special places and people for posterity. There is no panacea for time passing. But writing is one way to take action—and action beats paralysis any day in my book. (And, after all, this is my book!)

Chapter 7

Be Kind to Your Kids—
You May Need Them
<u>Someday</u>

Over time, the cycle of dependence revolves 360 degrees. When your kids are small, you are the whole enchilada to them. Then, almost imperceptibly, the pedestal you occupy descends, like a barber chair, until your total decline from omnipotence is complete. By the time they reach the teenage years, your importance in the overall scheme of things is relegated to, "Can you spare twenty bucks, and can I take the car?"

One of the problems with being a rogue, and having your kids (and their kids) know you were less than a poster child for propriety as a youth, is that when you do try to exert some parental or grandparental control, they laugh and quote your misdeeds back to you. As revenge, Dorothy and I like to tell stories about our children's misspent youths as often as possible.

Our son Graham was the athlete in the house. He was All New England in lacrosse at Kimball Union Academy, a cozy school tucked in the hills of New Hampshire. Later, at Curry College, he captained the Division III hockey championship team. They had a twenty-seven-game undefeated streak in the process. Our daughter Jenny was the student, who attended Andover and then went on to Trinity College in Hartford, Connecticut. Her academic achievements included Phi Beta Kappa and an armful of English prizes at graduation.

One was a voracious reader; the other used books as a door stop. They covered for each other. We're still hearing stories for the first time, though they are both now in their forties.

I was sitting at my Wall Street desk, staring at several screens, when the phone rang. "Hello, Mr. Rider. This is Dean Sylvester. Do you have a minute?" Sylvester was the director of athletics at Graham's college.

"Is he okay? Is he hurt?'

"He's fine, but there is a problem. His grade point average is lower than his points per game in hockey, and Mr. Rider, he's in a slump."

Well, at least he isn't hurt, I thought. "Dean, short of bodily harm, do what you have to do! I'll talk to him later."

"We've already taken steps. He's well aware of his predicament. He was placed on scholastic probation for the balance of the fall term. In the meantime, he'll be skating with a semi-pro team in Boston and we arranged for a tutor. That's the good news."

"What's the bad news?"

"You have to pay for the tutor, and he's expensive."

"Well, we'll make sure he understands that he'll be picking up the tab."

The wake-up call worked, and Graham's grades were never again a problem. Graham was elected captain of the team and was later nominated twice for ECAC (Eastern College Athletic Conference) player of the week.

Graham was and is a model of resourcefulness. Just prior to graduation, Graham and several of his teammates suddenly realized that they were deficient in accounting. Needless to say, his mother and I were not pleased. They all lacked the sufficient number of completed homework assignments required, and there was not enough time to complete them before graduation. They scraped together enough money to hire an accountant apprentice as a tutor, then completed and turned in the missing assignments. They all graduated.

While there have been many times Dorothy and I have had to step in as parental enforcers, there have also been many times that Graham and Jenny have left us bursting with pride and dumbfounded by their maturity and thoughtfulness.

Dorothy and I traveled up to New Hampshire to watch my son play his last game of lacrosse as a high school senior. After scoring a beautiful goal, he took off his helmet and sat down on the bench. I was afraid that he was hurt.

The school scoring record had been set the year before by one of Graham's best friends. Graham was going to room with him in college in the fall. Tragically, Chris had been diagnosed with Hodgkin's disease, and when he came to watch Graham's last game, he was thin and losing his hair from the chemo treatments. We realized that Graham had taken himself out of the game one point shy of Chris's record. Sadly, Chris died a year later.

During Graham's senior year, he received the coveted Headmaster's Award for the Most Improved Student, an impressive achievement considering that he and his buddies had spent their four years of high school living as spirited and fun-loving athletes, causing deviltry at every turn.

Happily, Jenny's voyage through academia was more tranquil, though it too had its topsy-turvy moments. In grade school, Jenny sang in the church choir. One spring she participated in a choral event presided over by a visiting British choirmaster. The choirmaster was a stern, no-nonsense instructor. The wife of Jenny's school principal was also in the choir, and she told Dorothy that the instructor had not gone easy on Jenny, despite her young age.

When we asked Jenny about it she said, "Don't be too hard on him. He's just old and bossy. You know, Dad, kind of like you."

A few years later, Jenny's halo evaporated and was replaced by tiny horns, tail, and trident. She was on her way to high school in Massachusetts, the same one I had attended decades before.

Dorothy and Jenny busied themselves shopping for a school wardrobe that consisted of a red blazer, a Brooks Brothers reversible raincoat, Fair Isle sweaters, and riding boots. This was around the time *The Preppy Handbook* was published, and Dorothy and I were thrilled that this look was in rather than skintight disco miniskirts.

Two weeks after we dropped her off at school, Jenny's entire wardrobe was voted down by her peers in favor of the black shapeless garments purchased for pennies at local thrift shops, the kind of goth-meets-sloth look that became popular in the late 1980s. Gone forever were the L.L. Bean catalog clothes. During our first visit, everything came home except the sweaters (and she only kept those because it was turning colder.) Some of the clothes are still mothballed in the attic. We continue to ask Jenny for a refund.

During her junior year, she begged us for ice hockey equipment for Christmas. We had already spent a small fortune on Graham's athletic gear over the years. "Dad, I'll never ask for another thing," she promised. "This will be my birthday, Christmas, and wedding presents, all in one." She was finally showing an interest in sports, so we went along with it, and on December 25, the equipment was under the tree. Several weeks later, she called to tell us, "I got cut from the girls' hockey team."

The coach told her that she wasn't skating; she was wobbling. Apparently, her ankles were too skinny and weak. Athletics were again relegated to the background, in favor of her true loves: theater, reading, and writing. The skates and equipment, as good as new, are gathering dust in the attic, next to the clothing shipped home for storage.

Five years after the failed hockey experiment, Jenny graduated from college. Our euphoria was mixed with melancholy, as we packed the station wagon for the last time and said our goodbyes to other students and their parents, paid one last visit to the bursar's office, and made one final tuition payment. This phase of our lives had come to a happy close.

As we were about to leave, Jenny shattered the mood. "Mom and Dad, I'm not coming home for a while. Two of my roommates and I have decided to waitress this summer."

"What? Where?"

"Portland, Maine."

"But Jenny, you've never been to Portland. You've never been to Maine." She shrugged her shoulders and looked away. "How are you going to get there?"

"Sally's brother is going to drive us in his pick-up truck," she said impatiently.

"Who is Sally? More importantly, who is Sally's brother?"

"We'll be fine. I'll call when we get there."

Crestfallen, we drove the packed wagon home. What could we do? I had some ideas but probably would have wound up in jail if I'd acted on them.

One evening early in August, the phone rang. "Mom, it's me, Jenny. The tips are lousy. I'm living on scraps and leftovers. I want to come home." So, on August 8, we picked her up in Portland. On the ride home, when I asked her what she wanted to do next, she said, "I don't care. I just want an office job and a regular paycheck. Even if I do end up tired, cranky, and twenty pounds overweight. You know, like you, Dad."

The moral of the story? I'd like to believe that, based on all of our parenting, delivered through hugs, lectures, late night phone calls to dorm rooms and post-collegiate apartments, that they will be willing to return the favor when we get rickety and wrinkled (oh, yeah, we're already there) and need a hand or a handout. Why do they laugh and look aghast when I say that?

The standing joke between Graham and Jenny is: Who gets which parent in the end? Both argue for Mom.

"I want Mom."

"No, I do."

"No, I said it first."

"But what about me?" I plead. The result is always the same: "Whoever loses the coin flip for Mom," they say, elbowing each other and laughing some more.

Oh well, we'll worry about that later.

In the meantime, we're Class A babysitters (for grandchildren), dog sitters (for granddogs), and plant waterers when they need us. I don't mind a bit, but I am keeping score!

Chapter 8

Legend in My Own Time (Or Is It Mind?): How the Mighty Have Fallen!

After retirement, it seemed that I, once the omnipotent family leader, had been relegated to a bit player in his own kingdom. It felt like I was one step away from being left off in the stands of our local football field with a six-pack of Ensure and a note pinned to my chest that reads, "His name is George. Leave him at the nearest VA facility."

But I showed my family that this intrepid rogue does not go down without a fight when I interceded in the design and decoration of a new den.

Dorothy and my kids huddled with the builder, "accidentally" forgetting to invite me to the project kick-off meeting. (This was interesting, I thought, because they had no problem remembering to present me with the bill.) Together, they agreed upon the scope and timeline for the project, the type of heating and insulation, the size and shape of the windows and skylight, the location of the electric and cable TV outlets, the type of wood paneling, as well as the patina and color of the stain. Even my eldest grandson got a piece of the action and casted his vote on where to locate my grandfather's antique brass ship lanterns, which hung proudly on the wall abutting our kitchen.

What did they have planned for me, the grand patriarch and *éminence grise*? I was put in charge of one decision they all assured me was "hugely important." I got to choose which side of the pine paneling would face out, the grooved side or the smooth.

After hours of consternation, I called them all into the room. Standing behind my mother's antique blue wing chair as though it was the podium on Oscar night, I cleared my throat. "I have made my decision . . ." You could practically hear the proverbial drum roll in the background. "We will go with the flat, smooth side of the paneling."

I looked into the crowd, fully expecting rounds of applause for my sage guidance and firm decisiveness.

My son was checking his Blackberry for emails. My daughter was filing her nails. My wife had turned her back to me completely and was busy measuring the new windows for drapes. Only my grandson was paying attention. "Any questions?" I asked him.

"Yeah," he replied. "Can I go watch TV now?"

I retreated to the pool to plot my next move. Swimming always helps me find my inner balance. Plus, when I'm underwater, no one can yell at me for having the radio up too loud or having coffee cake crumbs dribbled across my sweater.

Imagine my surprise two days later when I discovered that the den had been paneled in the wainscoting I had firmly rejected. Once again, I had been ignored and overruled. Just as I was about to explode, Dorothy pointed out that they had actually done one of the four walls the way I wanted. Then she proceeded to tell me that, by the way, they would probably add floor-to-ceiling bookshelves. The group was still deciding.

Outraged at having my entreaties once again go unheard, I slammed the screen door behind me and wobbled into the pool. I was speed walking back and forth in the shallow end when my strapping son appeared by the fence and stared down at me.

"Say, Dad, I know you feel a little left out on this whole home renovation. But not to worry. We have another, extremely critical project for you. One of vital importance not just to you, but to the entire family, the two Labradors, and everyone on the block."

I have to admit, I was intrigued. Finally, a job to sink my teeth into. One that reflected my decades of experience and proper place in the pecking order.

"Son," I said. "Bring it on."

"Okay, Dad, Here's the deal," he leaned across the fence and solemnly lowered his voice. "It's very important at this time of year to keep as many leaves as possible from sinking to the bottom of the pool. No one, not the dogs or the neighbors or anyone else, wants to swim in a pool that's dirty on the bottom. Your job is to stay in the pool for as long as you can every day for the next week and fish the leaves out. We'll take care of everything else with the new room and the builders. Are you up for this mission?"

Hmmm. Not what I had expected. I had hoped that we would strategize together on all the home improvement tasks at hand. Instead he tossed me a Styrofoam noodle and handed me the pool skimmer.

As the week unfolded, I sat astride my noodle like a blue-lipped, waterlogged infantryman riding his stallion into battle, brandishing the pool skimmer and patrolling the length and breadth of the pool. No leaf was safe. If this was to be my solitary mission, I would do it with élan.

Sometimes my grandchildren would venture towards the pool fence, curling their adorable little fingers around the chicken wire. "Poppy," they'd say, "You missed a couple down by the deep end."

"Watch this!" I'd reply, zooming to the other end of the pool. *Swish. Swish. Chuck.* I'd skim the surface of the water, retrieve the leaves and shoot them over the side of the pool.

Meanwhile, the other family members ticked off the various tasks involved in finishing the renovation. The builder's van zoomed in and out of the driveway. A rental truck pulled up, and strange men unloaded furniture that had long ago been placed in storage. Empty cardboard boxes for a new TV and iPod speakers littered the back porch. (Did we even own an iPod? What exactly is an iPod?) Buzz saws growled. Vacuums groaned. New track lighting blinked on and off. All the while, I bobbed up and down on my noodle, hunting down leaves and the occasional infidel frog trying to invade the homeland (or should I say "homepool?").

"Need any help?" I would offer occasionally. My voice, weakened by constant exposure to the elements, wafted over the fence to various family members who were busily darting in and out, carrying boxes and tools.

"No worries, Dad, we got it," they'd reply.

Over the course of the entire week, I patrolled the length of our pool countless times. I pulled muscles I didn't know I even had anymore. My red hair turned practically green from chlorine.

On the brighter side, I did get to hone my skills astride my noodle, wielding my lance like a weapon, and I lost three pounds. Should leaf chasing become an Olympic event, look for me at the trials! By the way, somehow, without the benefit of my superior input, the new room is finished and looks great! Best of all, my favorite chair sits right next to "my wall"—the king's throne in the newest corner of his fiefdom. Who knows, if I get lucky, I might even be allowed to sit in it! The lesson in all this? Relinquishing control as you get older is no easy task, but staying out of the fray—and avoiding all the attendant responsibilities—can be pretty damn nice once you get used to it! Now, if I could only get someone else in the beloved clan to pay the bills!

Chapter 9

The Dangers of Disobedience—Lessons for the Next Generation

The front door opened and slammed shut. I'm selectively deaf (my wife Dorothy often tells me, "You hear what you *want* to hear"), but even I could make out the sounds of tiny feet tiptoeing past my study to Nanny's kitchen. I decided to wait and let events unfold. A few minutes later, the clap of the pantry door closing was followed by a string of giggles, then more tiptoeing and another door slam.

The trap had snapped shut; it was time to spring into action.

"Who's there?" I bellowed in my best big, bad wolf voice. Silence.

"Hello?"

Nothing.

"Tory! Duncan! I know you're there."

Silence, then another string of giggles, then one child chiding the other, "Shhhh!"

I walked out the door and around the side of the house behind the garage. Four hands suddenly tucked themselves underneath coat jackets.

"Hi, Poppy!" Their faces were all feigned innocence and nonchalance.

"Nice try, you two, but next time wipe your mouths first."

My granddaughter and youngest grandson looked at each other and broke out into giggles again. Both of their faces were covered in black and white crumbs from Oreo cookies pilfered from their grandmother's kitchen. This was a strict no-no from their health-conscious, sugar-policing parents.

"Poppy, we're sorry," bleated Duncan.

"Seriously, you can't tell, okay?" negotiated his older sister Tory.

"Well. This certainly puts me in a difficult predicament, doesn't it," I slowly sounded out the words, making the wait to know their fate unbearable. "Come into my office and sit down. I want to tell a story." They looked back and forth at each other and I could see the thought bubbles popping into their adorably naughty little heads: *What's worse, getting punished by our parents or getting trapped in Poppy's office when he starts telling stories?* They deliberated and then decided to go with my option.

"Well, okay, Poppy, if we have to . . ." Not exactly enthusiastic.

"Okay, weasels, sit back and listen," I told them and began my tale.

Mom was pissed. I'd heard the word at school, but wasn't exactly sure what it meant. I thought I'd put it to the test, "Mom, why are you so pissed?"

That made her even more pissed. I guess my growing grasp of vocabulary was better than I thought. There was no school that day, so I had a whole morning and afternoon to amuse myself (and bug my mother).

Mom was entertaining her bridge group in a few hours, and I was underfoot. "George, I told you to go out and play."

My best friend Tim came over, and we decided to join a softball game down the block—in those days there were still empty lots—and then finish the afternoon off with some fishing.

We rode our bikes out to the bait shop, where I used up my hard-earned allowance to buy six bloodworms. Then we stopped home. Tim waited outside, while I ran into the kitchen and placed the damp cardboard box holding the worms on the top shelf of the fridge (or ice box, as we called it back then) to stay fresh. This shelf, it turned out, just above the tossed green salad my mother was serving for lunch.

The ladies began to arrive, one by one, ready to begin the fierce competition. They drank old fashioneds and everyone smoked. They would eat in another hour or so. The routine seldom varied.

Mother shooed me back outside again, and Tim and I took off for the game with our bats and mitts propped on our handlebars.

After a few innings, Tim and I biked back to the house to pick up our rods and reels. Just as I arrived at the kitchen door, I heard one of the ladies scream, "Jesus, Mary, and Joseph!" The wire-frame glasses slid off her nose.

"Is that you, George?" my mother bellowed. "Get in here. Now, look what you've done!"

I could see the prissy neighbor holding out her fork, upon which balanced a piece of bib lettuce, a cube of tomato, and, wiggling frantically at the end, a five-inch long bloodworm impaled on a tong.

The wet cardboard box had fallen apart in the fridge, and all six of the worms had found their way into Mother's salad.

Mother turned beet red, the veins in her temple looking like lines on a relief map.

I was immediately put into the equivalent of "Davey Jones's Locker"—banished to my bedroom for the rest of the day. Tim was dispatched home.

All I could do was wait, my vulgar verbal outburst that morning overshadowed by the disaster that had resulted from the wandering worms. I had been warned before about using the ice box indiscriminately. Dad was due home any-time. I hoped the train would be late—very, very late.

He was working long hours in the city for British Intelligence and was usually dead-tired when he got home at night. When he finally arrived, he came into my room. If I had any remaining questions about what pissed meant, they were erased that night.

"Isn't that great?" I looked at my grandchildren and let out a deep laugh, lost in the image of the testy neighbor with the bloodworm tartare.

"But, Poppy, you're supposed to be teaching us a lesson," Tory, ever the vigilant big sister, shook her head at me and scolded.

My reverie interrupted, I looked at both grandkids and smiled. "I know I told you this story for a reason, but I'm so old I can't for the life of me remember what it was!" I scratched my head.

"Don't worry, Poppy," Duncan climbed off the chair and gave me a hug. "Stay right here."

He and Tory padded out of the room, and then returned with the remainder of the box of Oreos in hand.

"That was a really good story," Duncan continued. "You deserve a treat."

"And we brought you some milk!" chimed in Tory.

"Well, aren't you the best kids ever?" We all agreed yes, they were. And we all dug in.

Chapter 10

The Weight Wars: The Battle of the Bulge

The older you get, the harder it is to take off the pounds that accumulate so easily. Trust me, I know. At eighty-one, I weighed in at a walloping 236 pounds on a 5'6" frame. It wasn't a pretty sight! One embarrassing evening nine years ago brought it all home. I was getting huge and had to do something about it.

Tale of the Tux

It was the eve of a gala at our performing arts center. The night was a warm celebration of community to honor Susan, an outstanding citizen of Bay Shore, but I couldn't get past the starting gate. The invitation read "Black Tie Optional," a choice I hadn't exercised in more than five years.

"Dear, help!" I bellowed down the stairs, panic ensuing. There I stood in my boxers. "This damned shirt has shrunk. I can't button the top button, and it's tight across my stomach." I removed the shirt and together we put the cuff links and studs in place. Dorothy deftly moved the top button as far as she could. I relaxed and eased back. I slid my arms into the sleeves. We both tugged and pulled until the collar button finally popped into place. My face was purple, my eyes were bulging, and my blood was barely circulating, but I was successfully stuffed into my tux, so torpedoes be damned. I adjusted my bow tie (a cheater).

Then the real fun began. I pulled on my pants with the braces already buttoned on. It reminded me of putting on my uniform on a Saturday football game day. The big difference was that the pants were not two-way stretch. There was no way to button the top button. Thank goodness Dorothy and I were able to pull the opposite sides together and fasten the clasp, but there was no way we were going to get the top button buttoned. "Breathe in, George!" Dorothy commanded.

"I'm trying, dammit!"

The cummerbund was another story. It was adjustable, but well beyond its appointed limits. I've always been handy. With the help of a pair of pliers, Dorothy and I made the necessary modifications and fastened me in.

The next hurdle was tying my shoes. I couldn't even do this on my best day. Thank God for Dorothy. She laced me up (hockey talk).

Now for the jacket. It fit snugly in the shoulders and tight in the waist. There was really no need to button it. This was a good thing, as there was really no way to button it either.

I was ready, as ready as I could get. However, another concern clouded my mind: How was I supposed to sit?

I strode into the lobby of the performing art center and was greeted by the honoree and some of the gala organizers. Almost in unison, they said, "George, don't you look nice."

I suggested that they move to the side lest they be injured by an errant flying button should I be forced to inhale.

The morning after, gone were my usual fried eggs and bacon. Neither were there any traces of butter, pancakes, waffles, or maple syrup. In their place, Dorothy had placed a sad little bowl of shredded wheat, 2 percent milk, and a banana.

"But, dear, it's not my fault," I protested. "I paid a lot for this tux, and the damned thing shrunk. I'll have a word with the dry cleaner!" Dorothy gave me that look, and I knew immediately I had lost the argument. I saddled up to the shredded wheat and had a spoonful.

Thanks to Dorothy, my equipment manager and keeper of my diet, I had made it to the gala in the appropriate attire. However, like all morning afters, it was time to be penitent and promise to hit the gym.

I managed to lose a few pounds in that round of the weight wars, but my battle of the bulge was hardly over. Five years later, my family did an intervention. We had moved to Essex, Connecticut, by then, and I'd become a regular at the local pub in the afternoons. The combination of the Black Seal's burgers and beer and Dorothy's delicious dinners had taken their toll. I had ballooned again and looked twenty months pregnant, with twins.

The Nutritionist and the Calorie Counters

The year I turned seventy-eight, I stepped on the scales at the YMCA in Westbrook, Connecticut, and a snide comment from my son Graham ricocheted through my mind.

A week before the Christmas holiday, my son Graham looked at me decked out in a Wedgewood blue sweater pulled over a white turtleneck. He shattered the moment by saying in a loud, sarcastic tone, "Dad, you look like an over-ripe grape in that thing!"

Enter my persistent, loving, nagging wife and daughter.

A chance meeting had occurred between Dorothy and a nutritionist named Tracy in a local bookshop. The trap was about to be set. Dorothy told Jenny. Jenny Googled Tracy and discovered that her credentials were impressive. Telephone calls took place out of my earshot. The game was on.

I was not confronted immediately. Instead, I was fed bits and pieces about the encounter with "the attractive entrepreneur and nutrition coach" who lived "just around the corner."

The soft-soaping worked. So did the photo Dorothy and Jenny showed me of Tracy. *What the hell*, I thought. Just going and listening couldn't hurt. I didn't have to sign on the dotted line. Besides, it would get the females off my back, and I was curious.

We called and made an appointment. On April 5 at precisely 9:30 a.m., a New World Order went into effect.

Tracy greeted us at the door and ushered us into her den. On the left was the dreaded scale, large enough to weigh a small elephant. She was very intelligent and polished and sensed my stubborn apprehension immediately. As her presentation unfolded, I began to warm to the prospect of getting back into my favorite shorts without blowing out the rear end. The logical simplicity of the program and her demeanor in delivering it had me taking notes almost from the beginning. Dorothy added to the answers I was giving about my lifestyle, eating habits, and goals. Halfway through the interview, I was hooked.

I was even inspired a few days later to ask Heather, the bartender at the Black Seal, for calorie counts on various drinks, should I decide to augment my arduous regimen. She told me an ounce of Dewar's was 64 calories, and a bottle of Sam Adams beer was 160 calories.

As prescribed by Tracy, we were to keep meticulous count of our daily caloric intake. (Dorothy didn't need to lose weight, but she insisted on going through the motions to help me stick with the program.) At each meal, Dorothy entered the corresponding calorie number into a log, which would be reviewed by Tracy at the next inquisition.

A week later, I had lost six pounds! The bad news was that the process presented some challenges. The following weekend, Dorothy and I were headed to open our beach cottage in Lonelyville for the season. Packing and planning for the six-day trip was consumed by our new dietary limitations.

The trip got off to a bumpy start. The absence of the usual Entenmann's coffee cake and my subsequent temper tantrum about running late rattled Dorothy. We screamed goodbye to our cat (who seemed relieved at my departure), hobbled into the car, and drove to the ferry in silence.

We arrived at the house on Fire Island around noon. The spring air was chilly, so I put the heat on and began to open up the house for the season, moving around seat cushions, plugging TV and light cords into sockets, hooking up my computer.

Dorothy commented curtly, "In your rush to get to the ferry, somehow I forgot two meals (a low-fat stew and chili) and the butter (fake, of course)." Her mood was dark, and her remarks were directed at me, not to me. I wanted to bark back but knew she was right, as usual.

We declared a temporary cessation of hostilities and quit for lunch, which consisted of one helping of Campbell's sirloin burger soup (130 calories), three wheat crackers (60 calories), and two Laughing Cow cheese wedges (70 calories) for a grand total of 260. After the "hearty" lunch, we put the rest of the living room together, made the beds, and settled in.

All was not yet connubial bliss, however. Dorothy had begun training me in how to count my own calories (a task I reluctantly agreed to take over). She didn't want to police and record every mouthful her beloved consumed for the rest of her life.

In preparing the paperwork for Tracy after a long day, I made the mistake of trying to recopy and record my notes on calories by meal and snack. I had trouble reading my own writing.

"Cucumber sandwich" was indecipherable, so was the calorie count at the end, and so it went. Each day's total was clear, how I got to it was a different matter. Asking Dorothy to help proved to be another misstep. She looked up amounts and helped me remember the items to be counted. The trouble was that the amounts and number of calories per item she calculated differed from my scribbled notations. The more meals we tried to track, the madder I got. After years of restraint, stifling the urge to use profanity in most forms (so as not to corrupt our kids and now grandchildren), my inability to properly add up my daily intakes sent me hurtling over the edge. I blurted out, "God Damn it, whose f---ing idea was this anyway?!?!" An hour of silence and the task was finally completed. Dorothy had resigned as statistician. "This time for good!" I was left to go it alone for the last lap.

That night we blew the count with spaghetti and meatballs and, heaven forbid, a second glass of wine.

The next day at breakfast, a pair of swans glided majestically into view in front of the house. I could tell that they were an item by the way they glided close to one another. They stopped from time to time to put their heads beneath the surface to forage for the delights below. I couldn't resist. I said to Dorothy, "I wonder if her highness is keeping track of *his* calories?"

Dorothy glared at me, and then said pointedly, "Don't ruffle my feathers."

By the end of the morning, I'd used up 483 calories, and I hadn't even gotten to lunch. I checked my count again: one glass of orange juice (85 calories), two cups of coffee with 2 percent milk (50 calories), one banana (88 calories) for a total of 223. What the heck? Then I spied a trail of crumbs by my computer. Oops. I had forgotten about the hot cross bun (260 calories).

"Dearie?" I called out to Dorothy. She came in the front door in her gardening gloves and boots.

"Yes?"

"I'm sorry I was a crank. Would you consider signing up again to be my calorie counter?"

She pulled off her gardening gloves, one finger at a time. "Fine," she said, "but no comments from the peanut gallery. Got it?"

"Thank you," I replied, down but not defeated. "Let's drink to it." I limped over to the kitchen and poured two glasses of milk, then reached to the top of the fridge for the rest of the hot cross buns, cracked open the box, and handed us both one. "But first, let's take the rest of the day off, shall we?"

Four years later, no surprise, my weight was still an off and on again issue (mostly on.) By this time, Jenny had introduced us to a wonderful guy named Bill McKeever. Jenny and Bill had just announced their plans to marry, when she smiled and gave me an ultimatum. "Dad, lose weight! I want you to be able to dance at the wedding. After all, you're paying for the band." (I was?) Dorothy and my son Graham seconded the motion. Bill, my future son-in-law, smartly pled the Fifth, as did Ladybug, our loyal Labrador. The next phase of my fight to get fit was underway.

Reaching Critical Mass!

February 20 at 1500 hours (that's 3:00 p.m. for you land lubbers!), it was determined that I had reached "critical mass." With my wife by my side, I was led into my internist's office, contrite and ready to take my medicine. I was ordered to strip down to my skivvies. I offered no resistance. I had not followed his instructions since last I passed through his door and had gained three pounds rather than losing the twenty-five he had prescribed. All other vital signs and blood levels were well in line, except for the blood sugar. The weight was way out of whack, and I knew it.

The fight was out of me. To compound my dilemma, Jenny's wedding date was inching closer. There were just four months to go before the big day!

The die was cast. Dorothy joined the physician and me and took notes at my inquisition. The good doctor provided his choice of a diet doctor with a telephone number.

Despite all the rough winter weather we'd been having, it was my bad luck that it didn't snow on February 25, the morning of my appointment with Dr. Slim Down. We arrived early and were greeted by a bubbling assistant armed with a fistful of intrusively detailed forms to fill out.

Halfway through this clerical ritual, I was ushered into Dr. Slim's office. I again stripped to my skivvies. A lifetime ago, I could have accompanied Rose La Rose at The Old Howard Burlesque in Scully Square Boston!!

The instructions flew. All the ingredients for the rest of my life (or at least until I lost forty pounds) were spelled out. The diet to accomplish my weight loss goals came through with depressing clarity. At the end of his soliloquy, I had little left but to ask him timidly, "How about an occasional drink?"

To my surprise and joy he replied, "You can have a glass of red wine with dinner."

My mind raced to the largest glass in the house. The attitude adjustment was still far from complete! The doctor's office was stocked with the requisite ingredients to make me thin or, better said, less round. We departed for home armed with two full bags of goodies, instructions, and an appointment to return in two weeks for my first weigh-in.

I ate my last hearty meal that evening. The bill of fare began with two gin and tonics, two helpings of a fine sirloin steak, a baked potato with cheese and sour cream, and a large scoop of vanilla ice cream with chocolate sauce.

I slept like a top until the day of reckoning dawned. I began my daily routine with downing five pills (for an array of other non-weight-related, old fart health issues) and starting my daily eye drop discipline—three different drops to alleviate the pressure from my glaucoma, dripped at different times, for a total of seven drops in each eye daily. It was like warming up in the bullpen!

I settled at my desk to write and watch the news. It was snowing like hell. I sat and pondered my fate: three carefully prescribed and measured meals per day, including morning and lunch "health shakes," three additional pre-packaged snacks, and drink ten ten-ounce glasses of water.

Dorothy called out from the kitchen, "Dear, your breakfast is ready!"

I took my seat at the dining room table. Time to kick off the new, no-holds-barred diet.

Dorothy presented me with a small dish containing three opaque fat burner pills (about the size of rabbit pellets) and four turbo-charged capsules that contained fish oil and additional fat burner enhancers.

My gullet was ready. Down went the seven pills and capsules with my second ten-ounce glass of water. Nine more dietary pills and capsules rounded out the pill count for the day.

Next on the bill of fare came a large chocolate, weight management milkshake. Not an English muffin buttered with raspberry jam in sight. I had to admit that the milkshake was really tasty.

My mid-morning snack consisted of half a nutrition bar with a capsule that prevents diabetes and a green tea mix in a glass of water. Lunch featured another tasty milkshake and a garden salad with vinaigrette dressing. My mid-afternoon snack consisted of the other half of the nutrition bar and a second green tea mixed in a glass of water.

Dinner was a mixture of vegetables and a protein, either meat or fish. The first night I chose chicken. A peanut butter diet snack capped off the day. *Where is my G&T?* I ruminated. *Where are the crackers and cheese?*

The combination of pills and capsules—fat burners, enhancers, multivitamins, diabetes preventers, and fish oil—was whopping sixteen per day. My water intake was one hundred ounces. Ugh!

To make matters worse, the word soon got around about my new health mandate. One morning, I picked up the telephone. The caller had a British accent and said that he had just heard about my diet and represented the manufacturer of one of my supplements. He asked me if I would fill out a questionnaire about the product and then proceeded to ask me a series of increasingly probing personal questions.

"What has my sex life have to do with any of this? What sex life?" I responded and demanded to know where he gotten my name. He said that he had received his information on Facebook. "Facebook? The only way I can log on to Facebook is if my grandchildren are visiting?!?!"

The voice on the other end of the line started laughing. It was my college roommate Richard Haskel, calling from California. He had learned about my dietary debacles from another close friend and classmate.

"Ha. Ha," I said. "Wait 'til I give his wife my nutritionist's number!"

My buddies weren't the only ones having a laugh at my expense. A few days later, I was peeling back the wrapper on the remaining half of that afternoon's nutrition bar. Daughter Jenny asked for a taste. I broke off a corner (a very small corner) and handed it to her. In the process, I fumbled the remainder. It fell on the floor, inches away from Ladybug's nose.

Ladybug quickly came to life (an achievement in itself, as she is also long in the tooth and somewhat chubby). She looked at what was left of my afternoon snack, stared up at me with her big brown eyes, licked her lips, and prepared to lunge.

It was face-off between two aging carnivores. The athlete in me took over. I moved swiftly and snatched my treat from Ladybug's open-mouthed attack. I popped the remainder in my mouth without even dusting off the dog dribble and damned near swallowed it whole.

Guilt set in, so I rewarded Ladybug with a dog biscuit for coming in second. She pawed at my lap for another treat, and I gave her a stern talking-to about dietary discipline. I told her, "Like it or lump it, Ladybug, this house is on food and fun lockdown until I can waltz at Jenny's wedding." Lady sighed, and I joined her. For a moment, I think we both hoped Jenny and Bill would just run off and elope.

I made it through the first day, then the first week and first month. Now I'm six months in. My sense of humor has improved. Due to the water consumption, I have firsthand knowledge of every men's room in a ten-mile radius. If I were a dog, my left hip would be dislocated from constantly seeking out handy trees or fire hydrants. The old adage that he "pees like a racehorse" has me heading for the fifth at Churchill Downs.

All that aside, how thankful I am that my loving family bludgeoned me into a health regimen that has paid dividends. I not only danced at Jenny's wedding, I practically jitterbugged.

If I can win the battle of the bulge (or at least stave off becoming a doppelganger for the Pillsbury Doughboy), then anyone can. It takes patience, discipline, and an army of loved ones blocking access to the kitchen, but you can win the weight war, too. Take it day by day, and if you slip and have a doughnut (or twelve), get up the next morning and start (or should I say starve?) again.

Chapter 11

The Wishing Well Caper—Watching Every Penny

The older I get, the more Dorothy and I count our pennies. We were diligent about saving over the years, but we continue to be confounded daily by how expensive everything seems to have gotten. A newspaper costs more than a dollar? A burger and fries will set you back fifteen bucks? What's wrong with this world?!

When nothing seems to make sense and the earth seems to have spun off its axis, I often take a few moments to sit back and ponder simpler times. Remember the days when every penny counted? I do . . .

My parents sacrificed a great deal to educate me and my younger brother Ken. Both of us knew it. We took any opportunity that came our way to make extra money. During my junior year in college, my lacrosse teammate Jim Ostheimer ("Osty") had signed a contract to sell a line of high-end cutlery and household knick-knack items for Hoffritz, a leading retailer in the field. He hired me to help him.

Rejection and how you deal with it is a large part of any undertaking, and life in general. Our first efforts at selling to roommates, teammates, and friends proved both fruitless and profitless. Most of them had no money either.

We decided to expand our territory and chose three destinations out of town to ply our wares. South Hadley, North Hampton, and New London were the locations of choice. It was no coincidence that they were home to Mt. Holyoke, Smith, and Connecticut College.

Between classes, homework, and lacrosse practice, there was little time left for capitalistic pursuits. Our selling trips had to be well-coordinated. Evenings were the preferred times. Research was also a part of our sales strategy. We plotted our northern forays during several meetings at our fraternity house, DKE, in hopes of gathering the names of girls at the various colleges who might want to purchase some of our wares (or alternatively accept our pleas for a date).

We loaded Osty's car with a full complement of top of the line knives, can openers, leather manicure sets, picture frames, combs, and other accessories. For our first out-of-town venture, we chose Smith. We headed north directly from the field house after practice.

We went from dorm lobby to dorm lobby, packing and unpacking the car. Nothing clicked.

Discouraged, we packed it in after canvassing four buildings. We decided to rethink our approach and stopped at a bar in North Hampton to debrief. The Marciano-Lewis fight was on the black-and-white TV. The bar was crowded with locals. Time sped by. Between the fight and our futile attempts to charm some of the comely ladies in attendance, we squandered most of the cash in our pockets.

It was time to head back to New Haven. Our spirits had improved. Osty turned the key in the ignition. "My God, there's no gas in this thing."

Between us we had less than three dollars. I remembered another bar near South Hadley a short distance away. We took off with our fingers crossed. A few minutes later we pulled into the parking lot of the Wishing Well, but it was closed. The well outside, however, was not!

We stripped down to our skivvies and waded in, breaking the ice as we bent down or dove to retrieve pennies, nickels, dimes, and quarters. Our total take was around fourteen dollars. There was an all-night gas station/convenience store located on the way to the highway, a short distance down the road.

All of a sudden, headlights appeared at the far end of the parking lot. What a sight! There we were, barefoot, barechested, teeth chattering, trying to put our pants on, and turning blue. We hardly posed a threat to society. Thank the Lord that the young trooper had a sense of humor. He could barely suppress his laughter. We received the obligatory tongue-lashing and the dire warning should we ever repeat the pilfering. "You guys take it easy on the way home. Don't catch pneumonia!" he warned us.

We finally made it back to New Haven, vowing to plan our next sales outing in greater detail and escrow a reserve for gas.

We all flunked Preparation 101. Had we had any success in getting dates, would the girls have watched from Osty's car as we bobbed for quarters?

Fast forward sixty-plus years. Dorothy and I are still very careful when it comes to spending money. And I still watch every penny—though now that I'm older and wiser, I make sure to do it with my clothes and shoes on!

Chapter 12

Boys Will Be Boys—
Keeping the Memory of
Loved Ones Alive

A great friend from college named John Phillips J.P. died away too early of a heart attack while attending the wedding of the daughter of a fellow classmate and close friend of ours in St. Bart's. Several years later, J.P.'s son Jim was diagnosed with colon cancer and was not responding well to treatment. At my daughter Jenny's suggestion, I began to write the story that follows for Jim. One of the greatest advantages of growing older is your ability to share your memories with the next generation—especially memories of their loved ones who have passed away. With every story you tell them about their dearly missed dad, mom, or grandparent, you give them back a piece of that person. If you take the time to write the stories down (and you should), you allow them to reconnect with those they lost whenever they feel like it, just by picking up the page.

But don't wait, like I did. Put pen to paper sooner rather than later, because you don't know what's around the corner—whether you'll be able to write the story when you finally get around to it, or whether the person you write the story for will be there to read it when you're done.

Tragically, the young man I wrote this story for passed away before I could share it with him. I'll never forgive myself for that. But the experience strengthened my conviction to be a storyteller and memory keeper for those I love and for those who love them. You can serve the same role for your loved ones. Just start writing and sharing. It's that simple.

For Jim

Four years of college went by way too quickly. The friendships formed lasted a lifetime.

My first encounter with your dad occurred at high school football practice late in the 1950 season, three weeks before the big game with our rival school, Exeter.

Names of our counterparts on the opposing team were stenciled on five padded uprights fastened to the blocking sled. I hit "Phillips" at least ten times each practice as the defensive line drove the sled backward until our legs could churn no more.

Had the good fortunes of the football gods shone on me one more week, I would have played opposite him. However, a blindside clip against a Tufts freshman the week before changed the script, and I was on crutches as I watched Exeter trounce us from the sidelines.

Fast forward to the fall of 1951 and college freshmen football tryouts in New Haven. The guard slots were hotly contested. My friendship with your dad started right then. I was one of the smaller entries, maybe the smallest. My advantages were speed and agility off the snap, both diminished by the knee brace and bandages I was forced to wear.

J.P., our buddy Richard Haskel, and several other "uglies," as the guards and tackles became known, carpooled daily to the field house for practice. During those rides, we got to know each other well through our youthful bantering, and I got the first taste of your dad's hilarious sense of humor. Unfortunately, I got hit again early in the season and decided to pack it in. I later underwent a successful knee surgery to remove the lateral meniscus cartilage and have a tuck taken in the lateral collateral ligament.

Three years later, J.P. was one of twelve juniors that Mom and Dad let me invite to our family beach house in Lonelyville for a weeklong holiday between final exams and our summer military training—some Army, some Air Force, some Navy. By then the friendships formed freshman year had become tight bonds.

Dad took a picture of us with my mother seated in the midst of what she called the "Beef Trust" (as opposed to brain trust, since scholars we were not). The picture still hangs in many of our dens today.

Our daily routine consisted of rugby games at the ocean with scrapes and an occasional bloody nose, and swimming in an ocean that was nearly perfect all week. This was topped off with great food and nightly forays into Ocean Beach about a mile away, the only community then with more than one bar and an abundance of action.

Our group had an advantage. We had our own piano player. Goldie's was the bar of choice. The owner was one of the great jazz players of his time. Our piano player sat in for Goldie during breaks. The girls crowded around him as he played, perfectly situated for the rest of us to poach.

The logistics of ordering and supplying food and beverages fell to Mom. Satisfying a dozen hungry and thirsty growing boys was no easy task. Daily trips to replenish the supplies at the local grocery store were handled by willing members of her "Beef Trust," while others eagerly pitched in making beds, sweeping, doing dishes, and burying the garbage (this was long before the days of Hefty bags and recycling). Mom was the perfect chaperone. She knew when to appear and disappear.

One night, several early returnees from Ocean Beach decided on a midnight snack. The next morning Mom got up early to make coffee. She opened the ice box door. Gone were three dozen eggs, two loaves of bread, two pounds of bacon, and three quarts of milk.

Dad arrived for the weekend and joined right in. J.P. was always his favorite among my friends. Dad was a master outdoor griller and presided over the planning and preparation of the early Sunday get-away lunch. Rumpled paper, discarded shingle slats chipped with his hatchet, charcoal, and a match—this was all the preparation he required. The meal consisted of eight porterhouse steaks grilled to order, three dozen ears of sweet Long Island corn, three cases of beer, salads, sliced beefsteak tomatoes, Vidalia onions, four apple pies, and three quarts of ice cream. The entire spread disappeared in record time.

By the end of the meal, the mood had grown subdued, partly because of our full bellies, partly because of the growing apprehension we felt about heading out for our various military training sessions.

Although the Korean War had ended, animosities still smoldered around the world, and there was still a lot of saber rattling between the U.S. and the Russians. While we felt safe and sound ensconced in our sheltered college life, active duty loomed just a year away, with no way to know what the global landscape would look like by then—and how much of our military training we might be called to put to use.

After graduation in 1955, several of the "Beef Trust" reconvened on Fire Island for one last fling before heading for places, responsibilities, and circumstances unknown.

One member of the group asked me to rent a house for his secret society to use for their post-graduation celebration. J.P., the piano player, and I took on the assignment. We settled quickly on a four-bedroom house in Ocean Beach with a guest cottage sharing the back deck.

The renters were not due until the weekend. The three of us decided to use the house for the three days prior to their arrival. Who would mind? Who would know?

Either the real estate lady was greedy or just plain thickheaded. No matter, I signed the lease and put down the security deposit. Unbeknown to me, the guest cottage had been rented to two young and very attractive divorcees. This had all the makings of a train wreck. Like raw meat and a pride of hungry lions, primal instincts bubbled up.

We moved in, provisioned the kitchen, and set about getting ready for our first night on the town. J.P. was the last to shower. The piano player and I sipped beers and planned our next moves. As J.P. emerged, there was a lull in our conversation. The unmistakable sounds of soft music and female voices came wafting through the thin sheetrock wall separating the main house from the guest cottage.

J.P.'s curiosity heightened as he approached the source of the sound. He cocked his head back and accelerated it forward, crashing through the sheetrock wall (fortunately there was no two-by-four in the way). There, before him in the cottage, were two half-clad beauties readying themselves for a trip downtown.

Startled at the sight of J.P.'s head sticking through the wall like some hunter's trophy without the horns, they screamed and squealed. The music stopped and one of the girls dialed the police number posted on their ice box door.

J.P. couldn't back his head out of the jagged hole he had created. We came to the rescue and broke more of the sheetrock in an effort to free him. It appeared to the frightened girls that we were trying to break down the wall entirely and enter their quarters. As discretion is the better part of valor, we decided to vacate the premises before the arrival of the local constabulary.

Now occupying barstools at Goldie's, worries of our earlier skirmish quickly faded. We began to enjoy the evening, oblivious to the chain of events that would unfold.

The police roused the ditzy real estate lady and checked the house. I had left my copy of the lease on the kitchen counter, complete with my name and my parents' phone number. (Like I said, we were more "beef trust" than "brain trust.") They also knew me from lifeguarding and knew my grandfather as the doctor who tended to the Ocean Beach community. Calls were made to my parents and Gramp. The girls chose to press charges.

All this time, we continued our merrymaking, moving from Goldie's to Flynn's in Ocean Bay Park. Each of us found lodging and spent the night away from the house.

The next day, I made a routine phone call home. All hell broke loose. "Where have you been?" my father roared. "The police are looking all over for you. You're in deep trouble. Turn yourself in. Call us right away. Your grandfather is on the warpath!"

Fortunately, the lifeguards and police had always enjoyed an almost fraternal relationship. I called them and said I'd be right in, assuring them that we meant the two girls no harm.

I arrived at the police house contrite but firm in the contention that the real culprit was the stupid realtor (a twenty-one-year-old's misguided logic). I offered to apologize to the two girls and assured them that I would personally repair any damages. The girls agreed to drop the charges. I called Mom, then Dad at work, then Gramp to offer a tepid defense. I survived three tongue lashings and a revocation of several hard-earned privileges. I knew that we had dodged a bullet. The fact that I was reporting to my ship in two weeks also helped minimize the severity of their reaction. The incident faded from the minds of the local authorities, but the memory stayed with me and your dad.

J.P. completed his military active duty before I did. He was well on his way to a very successful career at First Boston before I got out and started looking for a job.

I was lucky enough to land an interview for a position at the same firm. I was thrilled and called J.P. to tell him of my good fortune. He invited me for lunch at The Hargus, a quick-serve, top-of-the-line restaurant across from the New York Stock Exchange. I arrived early and seated myself. Your dad arrived. He looked like he had just stepped out of an ad for *GQ*. He was sporting a finely tailored dark blue suit, white button-down shirt, and a maroon and blue regimental striped tie. In his right hand, he carried an expensive-looking leather briefcase.

We shook hands. "What's in the briefcase?" I asked, in awe.

J.P. was one of a kind. He cleared his throat and that guttural chuckle that started at his toes soon became louder and erupted into the famous Phillips's laugh, filling the restaurant.

He looked at me sheepishly and opened the briefcase, revealing its contents: a softball glove, a copy of *Sport's Illustrated*, *The Fall Football Review*, and a bologna sandwich tightly wrapped. We both burst out laughing. I bought one just like it the next morning.

Your dad was a wonderful storyteller. Swapping them was a favorite pastime. He related one of my favorites on the back deck of your family's place on Fire Island. He began by saying, "George, you know how tough it is for linemen to keep the weight off." (Boy, did I!) "My doctor, Barbara, and the kids kept after me. I finally gave in last winter and signed up for a weight-loss program—twelve days at a spa in rural New Hampshire. Most of the inmates were women—women who had very little patience for a fat guy who hated to diet, missed his wife like hell, and kept whining he wanted to go home. That, plus the monotonous daily routine—up early, sweat pants, vegetable juice, more supervised exercise, skimpy, tasteless meals, endless nutrition lectures—it all began to get to me." His eyes lit up with a mischievous twinkle in his eye (the same kind of twinkle that he had right before he slammed his head through the wall forty years before and almost got us thrown in jail).

"One afternoon another disillusioned male inmate and I decided, during a carrot juice time-out, to 'break out' that night. Shortly after lights out and curfew time, we snuck out of our rooms, dressed in the darkened hallway, and made our way to the window at the end of the corridor, sneakers in hand. We looked right and left, opened the window and slipped out into the night, no one the wiser. We put our shoes on and trudged down the country lane about a mile to the main road. Our escape went off without a hitch! The strip mall on the main road featured a McDonald's. The staff couldn't believe their eyes. The number of quarter pounders, French fries, chicken McNuggets, and milkshakes we consumed in short order rivaled anything they had ever witnessed. To top it all off, we ordered apple pie and egg McMuffins to go and large Cokes to wash them down with."

J.P. looked around and started to laugh again. "We got back, opened the window, and slipped in over the sill— scot-free—not so fast. The hall light flashed on and there staring at us from the end of the hall was 'The Warden,' a sallow-faced, mean-eyed matron, lacking in many things not the least of which was a sense of humor. She screamed at us, 'Get to bed! We'll deal with this in the morning.' Like two truants reporting to their middle school principal's office, we received a stern lecture on proper decorum the next day. We were grounded, not expelled, but also not invited back the next year."

Half the fun of listening to your dad tell a story was watching him tell it. He always laughed that wonderful infectious laugh, shaking his shoulders up and down and nodding his head. Soon everyone would be joining him. Just thinking about him makes me start to chuckle and giggle. His friendship was one of the greatest gifts of my life. My memory may have lost something along the way. Please excuse any lapses or exaggerations. And please know that I am sure your dad is watching me as I write this and will be watching you as you read it, smiling his huge, room-full-of-sunshine smile, sending us his love and light. He was that kind of guy. So are you.

Sadly, J.P.'s son Jim died at age thirty-nine, just around the time I finished this story. He never had the chance to read it. I shared it with J.P.'s wife, Barbara, and daughter Julia, and repeat the story here with their permission. My dad always said, "You can count your true friends on the fingers of one hand." J.P. was one!

Take a moment to count your true friends on one hand. When you're done, write down the stories you shared for you and your loved ones, and for them and theirs. Be the storyteller and memory keeper for your clan. Keep the memories and the people who made them alive.

Chapter 13

Once Upon a Blizzard—
When Generations Cross
Paths

It was March 2005, and I had taken up writing. I had ideas for two essays and thought, *What better place than our little cottage on Fire Island to develop them?* I had already put the trip off twice to accommodate my platoon of doctors and medical appointments, but now it was my time. There's not much that comes between me and my beach.

"Be careful, Dad, you're not twenty-five anymore," my daughter Jenny warned.

"George, if you fall . . . the new hip . . . this time of year there's no one around to help you," cautioned Dorothy.

"Pop, the weather can be awful in March! Totally unpredictable," my son Graham admonished.

"I'm going anyway," I barked back at them. I'm stubborn, I admit.

"Fine, have it your way," my wife relented. "But take your cell phone at least, and make sure to keep it charged!"

Little did I know that in a few days, I'd be caught in a major ice storm, out of food, cold and alone, wishing for once I'd listened to my family. However, the experience would give me a powerful window into the lives of my ancestors more than a century ago. It was a trip I would never forget!

Five generations of our family have enjoyed the rustic beauty, serenity, rejuvenating powers, and quality of life that Fire Island affords.

My grandfather built his little cottage in the town of Lonelyville in 1910. He loved to come to the island to enjoy both the outdoors and his creative pursuits. Gramp and his wife had two daughters. Each married and had two sons. The 1938 hurricane carried the original house out to sea; only the fireplace bricks and stones remained. They rebuilt near the site in 1939.

The third generation produced twelve great-grandchildren, and so far there are twenty great-great-grandchildren. One house became four. The original cottage is now nestled inland behind three bayfront cottages, all owned by various family members.

Since I was a child, Lonelyville and the Great South Bay have always held me in a vise-like grip that tightens as the years go by. When I'm on the island, a calm comes over me that's difficult to explain.

On the morning of Saturday, March 5, 2005, Rosie, our cherished rescue dog, and I were sitting alone on the top deck of the Fire Island ferry to Fair Harbor, facing aft to watch the sun reflect off the shimmering ripples and dance across the water. The temperature was in the mid-forties as the mainland fell away in our wake.

Like settling into a favorite chair after a great meal, warm thoughts of my late winter writing expedition became my focus. Rosie and I landed and walked the third of a mile east to Lonelyville. My supplies were packed in two canvas bags secured to a two-wheel cart that trundled behind me.

Since Dorothy had been busy and more than a little miffed at me for going to the beach alone so early in the season, I had had to shop for my own provisions. Unchaperoned, I had skipped all the dietary restraints and headed straight for the frozen pizza, frozen lasagna, cheese crackers, English muffins, Entenmann's hot cross buns, and some canine treats for Rosie. Not a fresh fruit or vegetable in sight. Just the way I liked it

I opened the back door of the house. The air inside was dank and heavy, the shades were drawn. The thermometer in the living room registered twenty-nine degrees. My new hip ached from the long walk and the cold.

The first order of business was to warm up the place. Once I had flipped all the switches and powered up the radiators, Rosie and I took a walk to the ocean. There I sat on a bench while Rosie nosed around the clumps of beach grass. The sun was warm. *Could spring be coming early?* I wondered as I looked west to the lighthouse, then east to the jetties of Ocean Beach several miles down and beyond. There were no other people or dogs as far as I could see. For a moment, the feeling of invincibility the beach always gave me wavered. I pulled out the cell phone and decided to give home a call. No luck. Despite Dorothy's reminder, I'd accidentally let the battery run dead.

It was a tolerable fifty-five degrees inside when we got back to the house. *Time for a quick check with the high command*, I thought, picking up the house phone.

"Are you having fun?" Dorothy wanted to know. "Is Rosie eating? They say it may snow later in the week. Be careful! Call me later!"

I set up shop in the living room overlooking the bay and began to write. On Sunday and Monday, the pattern was the same: get up early, write until lunch, walk to the beach, and then write some more.

Monday night, I checked the weather on TV. The forecast had changed; snow was now predicted to start the next day. The weatherman also warned ominously about high winds. *I'll shoot for the 1:55 p.m. boat back home*, I told myself. That would be plenty of time to avoid the storm, or so I thought.

The next morning, I packed my bags, checked the house for the last time, and started for Fair Harbor, where we would board the ferry back to the mainland. Rosie and I got two hundred yards or so from the house when the gray sky suddenly turned *Wizard of Oz* black. The wind changed direction on a dime—south-southwest to north-northeast. For a few moments, a large calm area appeared between the bay in front of our house and West Island, about half a mile north.

The water was flat as a mill pond and eerily reflected a single shaft of light that fought its way through the low clouds.

The wind picked up from the north. Sporadic gusts soon became a steady blast. The mill pond disappeared, replaced swiftly by rolling, white-capped waves that began to pummel the shoreline. The drizzle that had started earlier turned to rain. Rosie was shaking next to me. We had gone only a short distance before the rain changed to sleet and stung my face. I tried to take a few steps forward but slipped and nearly lost my footing. My hip throbbed. I edged over to the side of the boardwalk and held on to the base of a telephone pole to steady myself and rest.

Decision time. Maybe I should have paid more attention to my family. Dorothy's warnings rang in my ears. I realized then that Rosie and I couldn't make it to the ferry dock. The walk was too icy, the distance to the boat too far. We retreated back to the house we had vacated moments before and threw the switches back on. I began to have second thoughts. *Why didn't I go home yesterday as planned? Why did I even come on this trip?* And then other, more troubling concerns came to mind. *What if the electricity goes out? What if I fall? Who'll come and get me? Who'll even know?*

I called home again. Dorothy was relieved with my decision not to try to make it out. Rosie and I had enough food for one more day.

The snow and ice were now blowing parallel to the ground. The picture window was icing as the snow hit the warm pane, melted, and then immediately froze again. During this storm, the temperature would drop forty degrees in three hours. I crossed my fingers and hoped the electricity would stay on and the temperature would stay at a comfortable sixty-eight degrees.

The wind was blowing so hard that last year's bulrushes were blown flat, their tasseled tops bobbing up and down repeatedly. The house shook so hard that the blankets I had hung to cover the hall entrance and stairwell flapped back and forth.

TV programming was interrupted with storm updates. I looked out the window. There were no lights on the bay or in any of the houses around me for miles.

A few hours later, Rosie was asleep on the well-cushioned wicker chair beside me, a warm throw around her, the edges tucked in loosely, with just her nose showing. My writing was complete. Dinner was over. One hot cross bun left for breakfast and a tin of dog food for Rosie, and then our supplies would run out.

The book Gramp wrote about his colorful life, *Doctor on a Bicycle*, was on the side table. I hadn't read it cover to cover since my Navy days back in the late 1950s. The first chapter, "The Keel Is Laid," had always been my favorite. It recounts Gramp surviving the blizzard of 1888 as a ten-year-old boy, stranded with his sister and widowed mother on their remote farm in Patchogue, a few miles from where I grew up and lived for many years with my family. I reread the following passage:

It began softly on a Sunday in March—toward noon with little more than a thin, gray drizzle. Three of us were at home, my widowed mother, my younger sister, Lotta, and I. My older sister, Alda, then sixteen, had gone to spend the night with a girlfriend.

The morning had been clear, but when the rain began to fall, I heaped up some cordwood at the woodpile. Late afternoon in the waning light, I could see that the drizzle had become mixed with large, wet flakes of snow. For a time, I watched idly through the windowpane, conscious of the comfort and warmth within. After a bit, I went outside and did my chores—fed the chickens, shut the chicken house, and brought in a supply of coal and wood. Then we had supper.

During the evening, the mercury plummeted as the wind howled out of the North. Lotta and I went to bed, but Mother stayed awake listening to the blasts of wind that leaned hard against the house.

I paused to think about their lives without TV, storm updates, electricity, telephone, and no one to check up on the three of them. Then I continued reading:

During the night, the driven snow penetrated and drifted through cracks in the window frame. It covered my bed and spilled over onto the floor. In the morning, we wasted no time getting downstairs to the warm living room. I quickly made the kitchen fire. Then we found that a mounting snowdrift had walled shut the west door of the kitchen, cutting our way off to the well. Undaunted, we turned to the east kitchen window, scooped up a wash boiler full of snow and set it on the stove to melt. After breakfast, we caulked the windows in my room to prevent snow from drifting in.

Our modern double pane windows and insulation would have come in handy, I mused as I sat cozy and warm while the storm raged on around me. I read on:

Under Mother's calm guidance, we worked smoothly and without panic, although we knew this was certainly a storm the like of which we had never seen before. During the day, the wind increased in volume. To keep the house warm, we shut off all the rooms except the kitchen and living room in which we had a large self-feeding coal stove with a heater pipe through the ceiling into Mother's bedroom, the only heated room on the second floor. So fierce did the wind become that the carpet in the living room rose in billows.

We moved the living room furniture to the most protected corner, behind the stove. Then with clothes horses and clotheslines, we draped off the corner and covered the carpet with rugs from other rooms to conserve heat.

My reading was interrupted by flapping, banging sounds outside. I turned on the outside floodlight. At first, I couldn't figure out what was going on. Pieces of wood were flying by the kitchen window and crashing into the boardwalk fifteen feet away from the house. Then it dawned on me that the lattice-work panels I had so painstakingly nailed to the pilings were being torn apart, strip by strip, by the savage wind. There was nothing I could do about it. I went back and continued to read even though the lights were now blinking off and on and making me more than a little edgy.

One perilous trip to feed the chickens a pan of hot corn, the coop almost buried beneath a large drift. They huddled together and appeared quite happy. Indeed, when I next saw them three days later, the little flock were none the worse the wear for their confinement.

But as I turned from the coop for the trip back to the house, the going was all but impossible. I was walking straight into the teeth of the storm. I made the woodshed and rested. The space between the shed and the summer kitchen formed a veritable wind tunnel, and the ground was a glaze of ice, swept clean of snow.

The wire clothesline connecting the wood shed to the kitchen provided enough guidance to allow me to inch my way to the safety of the kitchen. Mother reached out and clutched my hand and together we entered the house, securing the door. Three days passed before it was opened again.

We inventoried the food...

It was hard to imagine that Gramp and his family relied completely on what they raised and put away themselves for food. There were no grocery stores back then. Their inventory was as follows:

A barrel of flour, half a barrel of sugar, a firkin [about a quarter of a barrel] of butter, a big wedge of cheese, and a barrel of newly salted pork. From the beams of the back kitchen hung sacks of home-made sausage, fresh hams well-salted, a couple of smoked hams, and several strips of bacon.

On the floor stood crocks of pickles, chow chow [a kind of pickled relish] made the preceding fall, bags of home-cured dried apples, blackberries, and dried corn—all the output of one woman's hands. Buried in a pile of clean sand lay carrots, parsnips, cabbage, and beets—all grown in our garden by me with the aid of the man who plowed the ground. A barrel of apples stood near the cellar

door and on the floor was a firkin of salt fish—
snappers and porgies—I had caught in the bay and
cleaned. A layer of fish, a layer of salt—until the
firkin was filled. Food was no problem.

Their cupboard was a lot better stocked than mine and
a lot healthier. No frozen TV dinners for them! I wondered
how they kept themselves occupied while riding out the
storm. Gramp told me:

All we could do with the preparations complete was
pass the time as pleasantly as possible. We read, we
played Parcheesi, we listened as Mother read aloud
from the Bible. We planned meals that would be
unusual, and we kept warm.

In the afternoon, Mother made crullers, letting
Lotta and me cut little figures from the dough to
fry in the hot fat: men, dogs, and horses. We made
molasses taffy and pulled the dough into tasty sticks.
Cut off from the world, we had a happy day. Just
ourselves and Mother, so calm and unperturbed.

The third day passed as had the first and second,
the howling wind devils shrieking to each other
from house corner and eaves. Occasionally with a
rumbling roar, the snow would crash from the rook
like an avalanche, covering a window.

Going to bed became a ritual. I undressed in
Mother's room; that is, I took off my outer garments
down to my woolen underwear and socks but no
more. Then I put on my flannel nightshirt. To help
shut out the cold in my room where the temperature was below zero, we placed an extra feather
bed as a coverlet upon my bed, although I already
had one under my sheets.

The one last thing before retiring, Mother asked
us to kneel in prayer in her room. When bedtime

came, it was fun to share my cozy featherbed with my lively fox terrier who nosed his way into the depths beside me.

Abruptly the morning of the fourth day broke clear and cold, with only a gentle breeze. The sun was unexpectedly warm. The melting snow froze hard at night. The next morning, after seeing to my chickens, I put on my skates and sailed over fences, rode high on drifts and slid down valleys until at last the warming sun melted the crusted surface.

Throughout those four days and nights, we went about our small tasks with a pleasurable sense of excitement. We moved through the wild, white days and icy nights warmed by our mother's calm and absolute assurance.

Even though I didn't have them for company like Gramp had his mother and sister, I thought about how comforting it was to get calls from Dorothy and the kids. It was nice to know that they were there. Gramp closed his chapter with these encouraging words:

God was with us within the snowbound walls of our farmhouse. No harm could befall us. The winsomeness and courage flowed from Mother and have ever remained in my heart and mind!

I looked over at Rosie, sound asleep, her nose still showing through the throw around her. I let her out the back door to relieve herself before bedtime. The wind, if anything, had strengthened, and the house continued to shake. Only two of the five steps leading down to the garden were still visible. Rosie all but disappeared as she went about her business. I toweled her off when she bounded back through the door and then put an extra duvet on the bed.

I sat and watched the storm out the window. The water roiled, erupting in angry white caps. I could still see bits of wood and flotsam fly past the house. Thankfully, nothing had broken a window. Yet.

The lights flickered on and off, and then the house went dark. I felt around for the flashlight I had left on the kitchen counter and some matches. I lit two candles and sat back to ponder my next step.

I could move from the bay cottage where I was now ensconced to the old family cottage, which was set back from the water and had a working fireplace. But it would be a four-hundred-foot walk down an icy boardwalk in blizzard conditions and, with my bad hip, I couldn't take the chance.

Another option was to call Dorothy on my cell phone and see if someone with a four-wheel drive could try to make it down the beach to get me. Candle in hand, I searched around for my coat and found my phone. *You idiot*, I told myself. I'd forgotten to recharge it.

Hip throbbing, I pulled myself upstairs and fumbled in the dark, retrieving three extra blankets from the blanket chest. I limped back and spread them over the bed, then settled in for a very long night.

The house was insulated, but without working heaters, the temperature began to fall quickly. The portable, battery-operated radio gave me periodic weather updates. The forecast called for snow throughout the night; the outlook for tomorrow was now, at best, uncertain.

I tried to sleep but couldn't. My hip ached, and I knew Dorothy and the kids would be beside themselves, since they couldn't reach me on the landline or cell. I thought of all the storms I'd weathered as a kid, here at the beach and on the mainland, including the hurricanes of 1936 and 1938. I thought of all the rough nights at sea I'd experienced in the Navy. But despite all that, I admit I was more than a little scared.

It's one thing to be caught in a storm while at sea with your shipmates or at home with your family. It's another to be alone, over seventy, with a bum hip and no means of communication or replacing provisions.

I decided to sit up for a while. The news updates signaled no change. The temperature had dropped to the mid-teens. The wind was gusting to fifty miles per hour, causing the snow to pile in huge drifts. Power outages were reported throughout Nassau and Suffolk Counties.

Despite the extra blankets, I began to shiver. The house was bitterly cold now. Don't panic, I told myself. The words from Gramp's story came back to me:

> We moved through the wild, white days and icy nights warmed by our mother's calm and absolute assurance . . . The winsomeness and courage flowed from Mother and have ever remained in my heart and mind.

Calm, absolute assurance, and courage. If my widowed great-grandmother and her two small children could find the strength to weather a storm of such ferocity, surely so could I.

I thought of the three of them, alone and vulnerable, in their primitive farmhouse as I finally dozed off.

At 3:30 a.m., I woke to find the TV blaring and the lights blazing throughout the house. I could see my breath in the house. Rosie refused to get out of bed. For some inexplicable reason, she had nuzzled under the blankets and was by my feet. She'd never done that before. Maybe there was some fox terrier in her, after all!

The floor was ice cold; I could feel it through my socks. I turned off the lights, adjusted the heater and radiator, and jumped back into bed. I decided not to wake Dorothy. I'd ring her in the morning. Rosie and I slept through uninterrupted until 7:30.

When we woke, the wind had dropped. Snow covered everything. The beautiful white blanket was interrupted only by two sets of deer tracks. It was so still, you could hear the quiet.

Dorothy picked up the phone on the first ring when I finally called her. "Why didn't you call?" Just as I'd imagined, she and the kids had been extremely worried.

I duplicated the exiting routine of the day before. Rosie and I headed for the 1:55 p.m. boat. Walking on the slick patches of snow and ice turned the trip into an adventure of its own. Normally a twenty-minute walk, it took us well over an hour. All I could think of was how not to fall on my new hip. Luckily, we made it.

If I had not left the copy of Gramp's book in plain sight on the living room table during my previous trip, I might never have gotten to know my great-grandmother, grandfather, and Aunt Lotta as well as I did that day. And, although I'm reluctant to admit it, I might not have gotten through that long, stormy night unscathed.

Sharing our adventures was an unexpected dividend. I never met my great-grandmother; she died two years before I was born. Reading about her made me realize that Rosie and I would have fit right in. She would have clucked over us just as she did Gramp and Aunt Lotta.

Though one hundred and seventeen years separated our two storms, for several hours during that long night, I felt as though we were all in the same room, as though time had collapsed and different generations had touched one another.

Maybe somehow they had. My one-day blizzard on March 8, 2005, had occurred so close to the date of their blizzard on March 11, 1888. I thought it was eerily ironic that Gramp had been born on March 8.

I'm not a superstitious person. I've never used a Ouija board in my life. But I do believe in family ghosts, the kind that hang around as benevolent presences when you most need a little TLC. I hope when my time comes, I can visit the kids and grandkids and maybe give them a little comfort on a dark, stormy night.

Chapter 14

Crime and Punishment— How to Guilt Trip Your Kids and Grandchildren

My grandson Bradley is everything I wasn't at his age: smart, good-looking, responsible, and earnest. I don't know how we could possibly be related. However, I know he's mine because he shares my rabid love of lacrosse and is an inexhaustible attack man. Bradley doesn't often get into trouble when he's visiting us. He's usually the peacemaker. For instance, when there are only three ice cream bars left, he says he's not hungry so his other three siblings get one each. When Dorothy pulls up in the driveway with a car full of groceries, he's the first one out the door to lend a hand. However, no one's perfect, and from time to time he gets in trouble by monkeying around with the other kids, breaking a cup or saucer, letting slip the occasional bad word, or pinning his brother in a World Wrestling Foundation headlock.

When we do have to lecture him, he takes criticism much to heart, especially when we give him the famous grandparent line, "We expected more of you." I like to wait a few minutes, and then remind him that everyone messes up at some point—I practically made a career out of it. I wrote the following story for him when he's a bit older with this in mind . . . Let's call it "Letter to a Rogue-in-Training!"

Sometime during my third year in high school, I was the last player cut from the varsity baseball team. The season before I was on the JV, batting .428, and was called up to the varsity. I never made it. The night of my promotion, we were horsing around in the dorm, dumping water on each other from the empty chocolate milk bottles awaiting pick-up the next morning. I was dousing my roommate, and he responded in kind. Our two bottles met and shattered, severing the tendon in my right thumb. It snapped and recoiled, winding up in my wrist. Two days later I was operated on at Jamaica Plains Hospital in Boston. The tendon was reconnected, but I was out for the season. I could never again grip the ball the same way.

The prospect of playing JV again was not appealing, so my roommate convinced me to give lacrosse a try. I took to the new sport quickly and soon found myself playing on the third midfield. I could run and I loved to hit. I picked up the skills with the stick as I went along. The team was loaded with great players. We won the New England Championship that year. Late in the season we beat Manhasset High School in an exhibition game, despite the heroics of sixteen-year-old Jimmy Brown (the legendary Football Hall of Fame running back).

At the last game of the season, we beat our rival Exeter to clinch the title. Wins in lacrosse against them were hard to come by. The victory was sweet.

The prom at Rogers Hall (a girls' school in nearby Lowell) was later that night, and many of us had been invited. It was a fitting climax to an exciting day. A dozen or so of us loaded our tuxes into three vehicles that passed for limos and headed for Lowell, making one stop in Shawsheen Village. The car trunks were rearranged to make room for beer and other beverages.

We struggled into our rented tuxes, fumbled with studs and cufflinks, adjusted our ties, and reassembled in the parking lot to sample the stashed contraband. We were staying on the second floor of a beautiful old house rented out for the occasion. A Tara-like stairway accessed our floor from the lobby where we waited for our dates.

I had a blind date, and I'm sure she remembers as much about me as I do about her. It wasn't exactly a match made in heaven.

My teammates and I interspersed our dancing and socializing with frequent trips to the parking lot to savor the contents of the well-stocked car trunks.

Mother and Dad taught us at an early age to make sure that all the girls had an opportunity to dance. A combination of the hot weather, excitement from the proximity to so many young beauties, and these trips to the parking lot had "loosened" us up. It was time to put into practice the lessons drummed into me as a kid.

With all the aplomb I could muster, I asked the headmistress of Rogers Hall for a dance. I'm sure that at first she thought, "My, what a fine young gentleman."

The problem was, my expertise on the dance floor was yet to be honed. After all, I was only a junior. The combination of my mediocre dancing skills and the fact that I smelled like I had showered in formaldehyde gave me away. After several turns around the floor, I returned the head of school to her table, unaware of the consternation I had just caused. I was convinced that I had completed my good deed for the day.

We returned to our house for the night, tired and some of us a little tipsy. We continued to party well into the evening, minus the girls. The day's activities caught up with us and several newly minted New England Champions spent the balance of the night hugging the over-worked antique toilet with the chain flusher.

The next morning dawned hazily. The seniors assigned the lower classmen the menial task of cleaning the mess in the bathrooms while they busied themselves checking out at the front desk and packing the cars. We were left to dispose of the empties. Several of the seniors went straight to the limos, climbed in, and closed their eyes again.

One of my fellow mid-fielders filled two pillowcases with empties and hoisted them, one over either shoulder. I grabbed a third and shut the door behind us. As I rounded the corner, I heard a god-awful noise. My nimble, gifted teammate had tripped and gone hurtling down the long stairway, uttering expletive after expletive, as cans and bottles spewed before him. He landed in a heap just short of the check-in desk. So much for a stealthy retreat! Miraculously, no one spotted us. We repacked the pillowcases, loaded the remnants of the contraband into the car trunks, and headed back to school.

On Monday morning, we assembled at George Washington Hall for the daily school meeting. Under each assigned seat was a rack for holding messages from faculty, administrators, and coaches. I had a green envelope under mine instructing me to meet with Dean of Students G. G. Benedict after the school meeting. I looked around me and spotted several other lacrosse players examining the contents of similar envelopes.

Later, we all converged at G. G.'s office. Besides us lacrosse players, the group included the senior class president, the valedictorian, the editor of the school paper, eight graduation day prize winners, and next year's captains of lacrosse, hockey, football, and wrestling. My thought was that we were about to be congratulated on our championship win. Boy, was I wrong!

We were interrogated individually. "Did you have any alcoholic beverages at the Rogers Hall Prom?" Most of us confessed, no one implicated others. Parents were notified by phone and follow-up letters, and we were all placed on probation. Senior prize winners were stripped of their prizes but still allowed to graduate. The lower classmen were placed on probation for the fall term and not allowed to leave campus for the duration except for away games.

Mother, Dad, and Gramp did not explode when they heard the news. Worse, they said how disappointed they were in me. They left me to stew in my own juices. I had to live with the knowledge that my dance with the headmistress had triggered a call to the house where we had stayed. Her suspicions were confirmed by my tumbling teammate and the falling contraband (turns out, someone had witnessed him trip down the stairs), thereby prompting her to call our headmaster.

We did our penance, secure in the knowledge that we had 'fessed up, not knowing the consequences. Those who did not had to live with fact that they didn't, and, even worse, that we knew they didn't.

I know my grandsons and granddaughter are far too intelligent to ever attempt to pull off such a spectacularly stupid stunt (or at least get caught doing so). But in the event they do, I know they'll do the right thing, own up, and learn from it. A true rogue makes a lot of mistakes (trust me, I know)—but never the same one twice!

Chapter 15

The Right Rite of Passage—Put Retirees to Work for Our Young!

By mid-April every spring, the jury is in for college applicants. Across the country, high school seniors have been rushing home, tearing through the mail, looking for that one envelope that will determine the next four years of their lives and have a profound effect on their long-term futures. It is the college acceptance letter—the capstone of a process that has become mind-numbingly more complicated and difficult than back in the days when I was a young rogue and college hopeful.

Some get lucky and are accepted into the top schools of their choice. Many others don't fare as well or are not able to afford the schools they wish to attend. Even worse, many more will not have made it to this stage. Somewhere along the line, they've given up on their college dreams because they became overwhelmed by the overly complicated college application process—a Byzantine maze many students are forced to navigate by themselves, due to a lack of sufficient support and guidance from the adults in their lives, at home, or at school.

The saddest part of it all is the number of kids from economically disadvantaged families who give up. They're the ones who need and deserve the chance for success that a college education can provide the most.

There's no easy answer to solve this problem. But I believe there is a hidden resource available to every high school in the country—a group of people with years of education and experience who have hours of time available to help kids sort through mountains of forms and applications, shape their essays, hone their interviewing skills, and decide which schools they should apply to. Best of all, these folks will do all of this work free of charge. I know because I am one of them. And if you're reading this book, you may well be, too. We're called retirees.

Since I retired nearly two decades ago, I have had the privilege of working with a number of fine young men and women from the local high school in Bay Shore, Long Island, where I was born and raised and lived until my mid-seventies.

Through my alma mater, Phillips Academy in Andover, Massachusetts, I started a special scholarship program for underprivileged kids from the area to attend the prep school's prestigious and rigorous five-week summer school program attended by students from more than thirty countries. Our goal was to help broaden their horizons and better their chances to getting accepted at competitive universities. To date, thirty-two eager youngsters have attended, and twenty-nine of them have received more than $150,000 in scholarships provided by Andover. These students have gone on to Yale, Harvard, Cornell, Dartmouth, Columbia, Northwestern, Boston College, Swarthmore, MIT, Fordham, and Northeastern. One has become a very successful writer and producer in Hollywood; another is in medical school. They all have amazed me with their talent and spirit.

About ten years ago, my daughter Jenny and I became aware of a wonderfully talented young lady, Kelila Venson, who was then a seventh-grader. Thanks to the efforts of a dynamic community leader who started and runs an after-school program at the local community center, we began to track the girl's progress and made a commitment to mentor her. She was determined to go to college, but needed guidance, as she would be the first in her family to pursue higher education.

Kelila was an exceptional student, but her PSAT and SAT scores presented a problem, and math was the culprit. She attended Andover's summer session after her freshman year, which was a big help, but she wanted to work on her skills even further.

Through my sister-in-law Janet, I learned that Mt. Holyoke had a highly regarded summer math program. We did some research and made some calls. The young lady attended the next year on a scholarship and received glowing reports. We also worked with the local high school to ensure that she received the best SAT preparation. She improved her scores by 190 points.

Then the real work began.

It started one cold autumn Saturday morning at a local diner. Piles of college applications covered the table. Our young friend did her best to sort through them, while I pulled out an Excel spreadsheet my daughter and I had created that listed potential colleges, their advantages and disadvantages, average SAT scores for acceptance, deadline dates, potential alumni we knew who could write references, and, most importantly, the likelihood that the school would provide enough financial aid for the young woman to attend.

Since I had more free time on my hands then Kelila and my daughter, I was able to call the schools in the ensuing months to clarify our questions about student aid and application requirements as they arose. It seemed like such a simple task, but it made a big difference. Our young student had no access to a phone while she was at school and would have had a very hard time tracking down the information she needed otherwise. In addition to a challenging course load, she participated actively in many after-school activities and worked twenty to twenty-five hours a week in a retail shoe store. She simply didn't have the time to do all the leg-work herself.

The weeks went by, and Kelila worked her way through dozens of forms and required essays. Throughout the process, my daughter and I were there to give advice, act as sounding boards, and provide much-needed words of encouragement. The day that all of the applications were finally completed, my wife, my daughter, and I cheered.

That night, I stayed up late and jotted down some notes about the experience. I wrote about how getting into college today is so much more arduous than I ever imagined, especially if the applicants have no resources, no connections, no legacy leg-ups, and no other college grads in their family to give them advice. It is a painfully uneven playing field, giving privileged kids an ever-increasing advantage. Their parents can afford professional college admissions coaches, special tutoring, and one-on-one SAT prep. Their parents have the time and knowledge of the system to stand up for their kids, which can influence placement in A.P. courses, as well as class and teacher selection.

The last lines I wrote down before I went to bed that night still haunt me: "How many gifted young people don't get the support they need? How many kids get left behind?"

The stars lined up for our young lady. Kelila received twelve scholarship offers and was admitted to her first choice, Northwestern. After graduation, she has gone on to a very successful career in beauty and skincare marketing. We couldn't be more proud of her.

Her tenacity and many talents made it happen, aided by an enthusiastic guidance counselor. I'd like to think that having a committed mentor with the time to listen and provide support helped along the way.

It doesn't take much to help launch one of the many deserving young people in need of a hand. They just need a chance and a champion. Retirees like us can provide a few words of advice, a connection to a certain school, or just a broader perspective that can make a world of difference.

In return, these kids will make a world of difference to you. Helping kids has been my dividend. Their letters and phone calls to me are treasures more valuable than all of the Christmas bonuses I earned during my thirty-five years on Wall Street.

If you are retired or about to retire, think about getting involved. Your local school and the kids you help will welcome you with open arms. And your family will finally stop worrying that you're turning into a couch potato. There is no substitute for one-on-one participation—and the thrill of receiving a call from a mentee with the glorious news they're headed for college!

Here's an anecdote that illustrates this. A few years ago I was lucky enough to receive an award from my local chamber of commerce. My daughter Jenny introduced me at the award ceremony. In preparing her remarks, she spoke to a few of the kids I had worked with, and they generously shared their thoughts on the impact of having a mentor. One young man, Jemel Wilson, is an exceptionally talented writer. This is some of what he had to say:

After knowing George for over six years now, I realize there are countless things he could have done with his life. As much as he loved football, I'm shocked he didn't play for Notre Dame, because with the size of the heart he carries in his chest and the fire that burns inside his belly, they would've made a movie called *George* instead of *Rudy* . . . wouldn't even have to change the uniform, I'm pretty certain they're the same pad size.

He could have been backpacking, chopping through some jungle with a machete, or climbing some mountain like Survivor Man due to his unrelenting, never-give-up attitude, and how he's strapped Bay Shore's young onto his shoulders just to help us through and show us the light on the other side.

Or maybe we'd be watching him on ESPN, sitting across from Johnny Chan at the *World Series of Poker*, an ace away from bringing home a bracelet and a cool million beans. Only because he's not afraid to take chances and gamble on a long shot, like myself and many others like me.

I guess what I'm saying is God has blessed George with all the tools necessary to be whatever he wanted and do anything he wanted throughout the years, but instead he's spent his time, money, and efforts making sure other kids from the same neighborhood realized their full potential and went after their dreams. If that isn't deserving of Man of the Year, then perhaps we should redefine Man.

As you might imagine, I was moved to tears. I encourage you to take the time to mentor a kid. It could change his or her life. It will definitely change yours—for the better.

Chapter 16

It Doesn't Hurt to Look— Barhopping (or Hobbling) After Seventy

It was late summer in Lonelyville, Fire Island, about a decade ago, and I was sporting a new hip and indulging my newfound pleasure of writing. After three days of tablet and quill, my brain was fried. It was time to take a break. I got into my bathing suit, which fit snugly after all the inactivity. I splashed in the bay for an hour.

I felt good after the swim and an outdoor shower. I changed into shorts and a navy blue sports shirt and decided to pay a surprise visit to some friends who lived in the neighboring town of Atlantique. Atlantique was a twenty-five-minute walk along the ocean, and I soon found myself climbing the steps leading to their home.

Pat and Sue's four-bedroom house was nestled behind the dunes. Their second-floor deck ran the length of the house and was an ideal spot for the obligatory adult beverage or two at sunset. There they sat, talking animatedly with another couple, totally oblivious to the impending arrival of their friend from the west.

For more than two decades, Pat and Sue had been our next-door neighbors during the off-season on mainland Long Island. In the years that we lived side by side, a close friendship developed between us, despite a disparate view on politics.

A favorite hobby during election years was to sneak over in the dead of night to plant a GOP candidate's yard sign on their front lawn. Likewise, Pat and Sue liked to conduct midnight missions to post Democrat signs amid our daffodils.

Resting on a bench near their house, I brushed the sand from my bare feet, cupped my hands, and hollered, "Are there any Republicans up there?'

"Are you kidding?" was the reply. "You won't find any here, but you can come up anyway."

After one last G&T, I had a decision to make. I could return to Lonelyville and go to bed, or I could head further east to Ocean Beach and the abundant nightlife that awaited. For once, my legs felt good, no doubt due to the lingering effects of the generous G&Ts. When I reached the beach, I automatically turned left, away from home. The closer I got, the more the memories came tumbling back. I was an Ocean Beach lifeguard for five years during high school and college. The path to the bright lights and bar scene was no stranger to me.

The long walk from the ocean to downtown over the dunes afforded time for more flashbacks. Most of the houses hadn't changed. That was Claire's house. There, across the street, the Swedish babysitter had held court, and so it went until

I reached Main Street. It was teeming with tanned revelers and kids with ice cream cones, buzzing and electric.

Like a magnet drawing a pin, Goldie's beckoned! It was now called The Mermaid. Fifty years ago, I had been an occasional bouncer there. The lifeguard crew considered Goldie's our base of operations. There were numerous other bars and eateries, but none with the appeal of Goldie's.

On any given night, customers might hear Vic Damone or Eddie Fisher, Georgia Gibbs, or Ethel Merman sing along with Goldie at the piano. Steve Allen often sat in for him.

The closer I got to Goldie's, the quicker my pace. Any lingering twinge in my hip was lost in the anticipation. My old swagger had returned.

The place had changed little inside. The piano was missing, but not the image of Goldie's hands racing back and forth over the keyboard or the wondrous sounds he produced.

The other major difference was the bar. Although it was still in the same place on the north side, rolled-up garage-like doors had replaced the solid wall, allowing the bartender to service bar and restaurant customers and at the same time fill orders for those customers preferring outdoor dining and drinking.

The bartender was a human octopus. This early evening, I was the only one at the bar. The real action was on the deck. The sun was dropping like an orange-tinged red balloon, into a bank of reddening cotton-candy clouds. The young blonde waitresses, their ponytails bobbing, were darting from the kitchen to the deck and back and forth from the bar. It was quiet inside. Outside, everyone was talking at once. I longed for the sound of the piano, and Goldie playing his signature arrangement of "Old Man River." The canned music was no substitute.

My reverie was interrupted as one by one, sometimes in pairs, the stools around me began to fill.

Before long, I counted fourteen tanned and shapely young women—some standing, some seated—all ordering drinks at once. I thought I had died and gone to heaven. I began to think that all of them coveted my company.

Of such occasions, my grandfather used to say well into his eighties, "Bird, oh, bird in thy flight, make me a boy again, just for tonight."

Back when I was lifeguarding, we would have been all over them. Instead, I engaged in polite conversations with the women and told the bartender stories of the past in between his order-taking.

Eleven o'clock and time for the long walk home. The running conversation with the bartender and the history lesson about Goldie's past so fascinated him that he refused to give me a tab. Even better, he gave me a "Mermaid" champagne glass as a memento. I'd have to hide it well from the family! I said my goodbyes to the girls and the bartender, and took the water taxi home. I may not be the lady killer I once was, but senior citizen barhopping was a hell of a lot of fun. I always say, it doesn't hurt to look!

Chapter 17

One Tough Cookie—
Helping Loved Ones
Through Challenges

Snap! Crack! It was one week before Christmas 2011, and I was gathering twigs and branches around the yard to use as kindling. As I did this, I was thinking about my grandson's upcoming operations that would take place more than a thousand miles away at a special medical clinic in Florida.

Graham Jr. was born with a condition called achondroplasia, which is a form of dwarfism. He had already undergone a few operations to add inches to his height.

Each time I snapped a twig or a small branch, the sound made me wince. I couldn't help thinking of Graham's bones being splintered during the operations.

In actuality, the surgeon—regarded as the top in his field in performing this procedure—would cut rather than break the upper and lower bones in each of Graham's legs and then insert metal pins or screws above and below the cut before stitching the incision closed. A medical device called a fixator would be attached to the pins in the bone and adjusted by the use of a wrench to widen the gap of the break while Graham's body slowly generated new bone. The whole process took place over several very challenging months. Every day Graham had to turn the pin to stretch his bones and skin, a painful and emotionally draining routine.

After Graham's operation, he'd have to stay in the hospital for a week or more. Afterwards, frequent visits to the doctor and a physical therapist would be required to adjust the fixator, watch for infection, and help Graham maintain his normal range of motion. All of this meant that Graham and one of his parents would have to stay near the hospital in Florida for several months.

Although the procedure I've described conjures images of medieval torture devices, Graham's doctor has had amazing results with this operation.

From the time Graham's fixator was removed after his first operation in 2009, all of us knew that the day would come when he would again journey to Florida. In the months leading up to the surgery, part of my job description as grandfather had been to drive Graham to middle school on a daily basis. The only sign of anxiety he revealed to me on our daily commute was when he said, "Poppy, do you know that this will be the first winter since I was born that I won't see any snow?"

Despite any concerns we may have had about Graham, Christmas was a joyous occasion. Graham's other grandparents came up from Long Island, and my daughter Jenny buzzed in and out from Westport, Connecticut. All the while my daughter-in-law Paulette was packing and planning for their five-month stay in Florida.

December 27 dawned. At first light, I looked out of my den window to see my son Graham Sr. busily putting the last baggage in the carrier atop their SUV. The tailgate was open, and Paulette was stowing a cooler and Graham Jr.'s wheelchair (saved from his previous surgery and soon to be put back into use) neatly in the back. Graham Jr. carried a small bag with movies, snacks, and books for the long drive.

My son and his wife were taking all four of their kids down to Florida to be with Graham Jr. before and immediately after the surgery. Later, Graham Sr. and the three younger children would make their way back to Connecticut for the kids to return to school. By 10:00 a.m., they were all packed and ready to go. I stayed out of the way, as the last thing any of them needed was a doting, anxious grandfather underfoot. Graham Jr. gave me a big hug and said, "Poppy, my goal is to be back in time for your eightieth birthday party."

I hugged him and stood back with Dorothy as we watched them leave. I have to say that the hardest part about growing older and being a grandparent is the powerlessness you feel when someone in your family is sick or in trouble, and you can't jump in and fix it, no matter how much you wish you could.

Later that week, we drove Jenny to the airport to catch her flight to Florida. She would accompany Graham's younger siblings back to Connecticut so they could return to school. Both sets of grandparents would take turns caring for them while Graham Sr. stayed in Florida for a few weeks to help Paulette. After that, Paulette would remain in Florida for several months as Graham went through rehab. Each family member had a role to play, and it was all carefully orchestrated by my son and his wife.

When Graham Jr. first started this course of treatment, his doctor had told his parents, "If you're going to do this, you will need your family to help you through it." Over time, this has become more apparent. It truly is a family affair. The generosity from neighbors and friends has also been key to the effort. The hero of course is Graham Jr. His courage and stoicism know no bounds. The rest of us are bit players, all eager, willing, and grateful to play our parts.

In June 2013, Graham and his parents departed for Florida again for his third surgery, this time on his upper arms. The bones were severed and external adjustable fixators were placed to facilitate the lengthening process. In short order, Graham was totally mobile and running around carefully with the fixators in place. What a tough cookie he is. And what a family he has.

I still wish I was fifty years younger so I could do more to assist during this grueling process, but I do what I can and hope that all of my grandparental love, support, and prayers help just a little bit.

Chapter 18

Say Thanks to a Veteran—Five Degrees from No Return

For my eightieth birthday, Jenny gave me a sharp-looking navy windbreaker bearing the name and likeness of one of the destroyers I served on embroidered on the back, and my name and rank on my left chest. I like to wear it when I do my errands, often with a navy baseball hat with USS *Abbot* embellished on it in gold print. For me, showing the world I am a veteran helps me honor the role the military plays in protecting our country, while also honoring those courageous men and women who have fought and died to protect our freedom. Once in a while, when I'm puttering around town or sitting at my favorite bar stool at the Black Seal, someone will approach me, thank me for my service, and even buy me a round.

For a veteran, this spirit of appreciation is warmly welcomed. What's even better is to share your time with veterans. You'll make their day and you'll carry their stories with you.

When I'm lucky enough to run across a young person who asks me about my service, I like to tell him or her a story about the day my ship was nearly lost at sea.

Have you ever been scared out of your wits? For more than an instant one afternoon in the spring of 1956, I was. We were scheduled to begin anti-submarine warfare exercises in the Atlantic off Bermuda with a convoy of replenishment ships.

The sea grew angrier as we moved south from Newport, Rhode Island. A hurricane had been tracking lazily north-northwest from the Caribbean, changing direction without notice. Not by design, we were heading directly for it. No matter what course we tried, the storm seemed to counter until we were being pounded.

We were in the middle of it. I was officer of the deck on the evening watch. I had relieved Gene McGovern, the operations officer. Next to Captain W. W. De Venter (or "WWD" to us), he was the second-best ship handler aboard. Gene had been on the bridge for ten straight hours. WWD had moved to his sea cabin, just aft of the bridge, as the sea conditions worsened. He spent most of the time seated in his swivel chair located in the most forward part of the wheelhouse, where he had an unobstructed view over the bow.

We were operating with seven other destroyers, a squadron consisting of two divisions of four ships each. The squadron commander, with the rank of captain, was located on the lead destroyer. We were arrayed in a line with proper spacing between the eight of us. Movement about the ship was precarious, to say the least.

A Fletcher-class destroyer, which ours was, has a break (an open space) on the main deck amid ship between the superstructures fore and aft; both are linked one level above by an open deck connecting the two superstructures, known as the 01 level. The only protected access from bow to stern was below the main deck. The sea state was so treacherous that WWD ordered the water-tight doors connecting the below deck spaces to be lugged shut.

Only men in the forward sections of the ship had sheltered access to the bridge. For twenty hours, the men quartered in the aft part of the ship, mainly engineers, had no access to the bridge and were relegated to their spaces with no hot food. Movements on the main and 01 decks were out of the question.

My friend and shipmate Ted Karras was "Boatswain of the Watch," which meant he directed the lookouts, helmsman, lee helmsman, quartermasters, radioman, and backups. I had the con, which is Navy speak for being responsible for the ship and its movement for a four-hour shift. The captain was either on the bridge or in earshot of the activity in his sea cabin. The squadron commander, located on the lead destroyer, gave directions for course and speed. We were third in line, heading straight into the waves. I was braced in the open shell door leading to the starboard wing of the bridge. The ship was climbing mountainous seas and then crashing down to the troughs. We were steering 040° and our speed was twelve knots.

Crackling over the radio came the order, "Change course, come to 130, speed fifteen knots."

I grabbed the mike and acknowledged receipt of the order. I repeated the order to the helmsman and the lee helmsman. "Right full rudder, come to course 130. Make turns for fifteen knots."

The captain came racing to the wheelhouse. Ted announced, "The captain is on the bridge." WWD came bursting through the shell door past me and moved to the outer end of the open starboard wing of the bridge to assess the sea state, just as we were slowly coming to the new heading.

The order never should have been given. We were lumbering into the trough, now parallel between two huge waves. We were thrown over on our side. I lost my grip on the knife-edge of the shell door and hurtled out as the ship rolled steeply to starboard, piling on to the captain who was clinging to the alidade (a navigational device) bolted to the deck, on the outer part of the starboard wing of the bridge. I've never been so scared in my life.

We held on side by side as the ship continued to roll further and further until it seemed like we could reach down and touch the boiling sea reaching up to us. It was angry and black, fizzing like a glass of Guinness freshly poured. Finally, we stopped. The ship shivered and shook. We laid there for what seemed an eternity. Slowly, ever so slowly, we began to come back. We had come within five degrees of capsizing.

We later learned that we had rolled sixty-three degrees— five degrees from no return. Had we not been properly ballasted, this story might never have been written. A capsizing angle calculation, called the "righting moment," takes into account the ship's center of gravity and ballast. At sixty-eight degrees, we would have had it!

WWD screamed over the roar of the sea, "I have the con!" thereby relieving me on the spot. As we continued to recover, he inched his way into the wheelhouse and gave orders to return us to a course heading into the waves, at the same time adjusting speed to enable us to maneuver more easily in the treacherous seas.

He grabbed the radio mike and bellowed into it: "What are you doing? Are you trying to sink us? I'll take care of my ship. We are steering independently and suggest you do the same until we work out of this." He slammed the mike back into its cradle. We resumed our course. The violent motions of the ship were no longer as severe. "Mr. Rider has the con."

The engineer on watch had blood spurting from a gash on the right side of his neck. Ted and WWD were trying to undo the metal chest-plate fastened around his neck that had been thrust upward when the ship rolled and he was thrown through the shell door. The wire connecting the speaker on the metal plate to the power source had snapped taut, causing the cut. They finally freed him and two sailors took him below for repairs, which required a total of twenty-one stitches. The gunnery chief broke four ribs when he was thrown against a bulkhead in the chief's quarters and one of the seamen in my division, off watch, suffered a concussion when he fell and banged his head on a table in the mess hall.

We and the next two destroyers behind us took water down our stacks.

No one aboard that day will forget that hour and what almost happened. Ted and I had more than a bird's-eye view of the adventure. WWD was never reprimanded for disobeying orders, and we all lived to tell the tale. WWD was much loved and admired by the entire crew. His actions that day added to his legacy. He had survived Pearl Harbor as an ensign taking a destroyer to sea in the midst of the Japanese attack, and he was on the bridge of the battleship *Arkansas* on D-Day. He told us later that surviving that storm was as memorable as anything that he had experienced in his wartime career.

As an avowed rogue and spinner of tales, most of my stories end with a wink and a smile. When I tell this one, however, I always finish with a huge sigh of relief and a thankful hat tip to the heavens.

Chapter 19

A Bloody Good Yarn—
Baalbek, the Roadblock,
and the Belly Dancer

I like to believe that when I write I always try to impart a deeper meaning, to connect with my audience, and share something of my experiences that can add a little light or perspective to their lives. After all, isn't that what a writer is supposed to do? But the truth is, I'm part Irish. And that means I am genetically conditioned to spin a good yarn, if I'm lucky enough, while sitting on a well-worn barstool. In the spirit of telling tales and revisiting one's youthful exploits, here is a story I'm including for no good reason—except that it's fun and, like I said, I have a lot of Irish in me.

It was early January 1957. The Christmas and New Year's holidays were over, and my brother Ken, our shipmates, and I were enjoying a great ten-day interlude anchored off Cannes, France. It was a well-deserved break. We had spent all but a few days at sea since leaving Newport two months before. The time went by far too quickly, and soon we put back to sea and joined units of the 6th Fleet and allied Navies conducting extended anti-submarine warfare exercises. At the completion of our duties, we proceeded on to Beirut, Lebanon, for a five-day stay alongside the largest pier in the harbor, where this tale really takes off. Joining us in Beirut was the USS *Hale*, another destroyer in our division. The pier accommodated both of us on the left side. We were first in and closest to shore.

But this time our break proved to be anything but routine! I had the duty first night. My brother Ken and several others went into town. At breakfast the next morning, the conversation centered on the Kit Kat Club and a belly dancer, who was reportedly the best in the eastern Mediterranean.

During the night, a Russian freighter docked opposite the *Hale* down the pier and catty-cornered aft of us. The wind was blowing from their starboard quarter toward our port bow. Their stack was billowing thick black smoke, the residue collecting on our deck, which our guys had just swabbed. Not a very friendly thing to do.

That night, I went ashore and headed straight for the Kit Kat Club. We had a great night, but with no belly dancer in sight. The next morning, Ken, assigned to the engineering department, notified me that the wind had changed direction and was now blowing in the direction of the Russian ship. He had arranged with his chief to return the favor and suggested that I go on deck and watch the fun. Our guys produced even thicker black smoke that billowed and belched soot all over the Russian ship. Their sailors shook their fists at us, and we simply waved back. Revenge was sweet!

As recreation officer, I had arranged a day's outing by bus to view the ancient ruins at Baalbek situated in the Beqaa Valley. Twenty crew members signed up. My brother Ken joined us.

Several of the guys purchased cases of beer for the trip, iced it in large buckets, and stowed them aboard the back of the bus. The ship's cooks supplied sandwiches. We left early from the pier and drove the eighty-five kilometers on a hilly route through the countryside to view the ruins of the temples, a treasure counted among the wonders of the world. I even rode a camel, much to the delight of all present.

On the return trip, the road took us close to the Syrian border. Ken and I were seated side by side in the back of the bus by the beer. The Syrians had set up a roadblock near the border and ordered our driver to stop, and all of us to exit the bus. Our driver spoke English and got in an argument with the scruffy local.

Ken said to me, "You're senior. You handle this. I'll guard the beer!"

Our driver said to me, "Under no circumstances let anyone off this bus!"

I stood behind him as he acted as mediator. Two more scruffy locals boarded the bus brandishing Kalashnikov rifles.

The driver told me that they were after the film in our cameras. They went up and down the aisle collecting the film. That seemed to satisfy them, and they left the bus.

I was pissed about losing a whole roll of pictures taken at sea and Baalbek. Ken looked at me with a grin and produced a roll of film. In the confusion he had replaced the full one with a blank and placed it inside his shirt.

The last day of our stay we were scheduled to depart at noon. Breakfast was interrupted when the *Hale's* skipper appeared in our wardroom. Our captain excused himself and both of them left abruptly. A half hour later, the squawk box announced, "Ensign George Rider, report to the captain!"

The captain and the executive officer were seated when I arrived. They wasted no time with lengthy explanations but wanted to tell me that the mystery of the missing belly dancer from the Kit Kat Club had been solved!

The *Hale*'s captain had asked our captain (WWD) for help in retrieving one of his young officers before the noon departure. The *Hale*'s officer had gone ashore the first night and endeared himself to Sophia, the gyrating star at the Kit Kat, and neither had surfaced since. To avoid undue attention on the *Hale* he had asked WWD to help retrieve his officer.

In the middle of this explanation, First Class Boatswain's Mate J.J. Cunningham appeared carrying two .45 pistols, extra clips, and a billy club. Our executive officer had already contacted the local Beirut police, who had in turn found Sophia's address. I was to be in charge of the "rescue" mission. J.J. had chosen the toughest sailor in the deck division to accompany us. This was Nick "Ski" Snigorski who was six-foot-four and 235 pounds.

WWD told me to get in and out quickly and with as little fanfare as possible. There was to be no force unless absolutely necessary. He wished us well. Ski was waiting for us on the dock. J.J. and I were armed with the .45s. J.J. handed the billy club to Ski just as two police cars screeched to a halt on the pier close to us. The three of us got in.

Twenty minutes later, after a drive through downtown Beirut, we arrived in the Arab quarter and pulled up behind the marked car carrying five uniformed police, who were already taking station in front of and around an apartment house in the middle of a crowded street. The police captain spoke excellent English. We conferred and decided that the three of us from the *Abbot* would make the first contact, with the others as back-up. J.J. and I went into the chambers and proceeded to climb the steps to the two-story walk-up with Ski close behind.

I knocked on the door. No answer. I waited and knocked again. It opened. There before me was Sophia, the best belly dancer in the Eastern Mediterranean, scantily clad and looking none the worse for wear. Not so *Hale*'s errant ensign. He was seated on a large sofa in his skivvies, unshaven, and too tired to be defiant. I called him by name and told him to get dressed and come with us. His ship was due to depart in under two hours. He replied that he had no intention of leaving and told me to "butt out." Sophia was still in the doorway.

I responded, "You're coming with us, one way or another! If you stay, think about it. You will be subject to Lebanese justice and a U.S. court-martial for desertion. Right now, no charges have been pressed, and I'll overlook your first reaction. Now put your pants on, shape up, and get moving. You have five minutes."

I stepped back. Sophia stepped back. The door was still open. The sight of me, J.J. and Ski towering over him did not go unnoticed by the ensign. Slowly he got up, disappeared into another room, and returned buckling his belt and tucking in his shirt. He mumbled something to Sophia, kissed her, and brushed by me. J.J. and Ski escorted him to the car and sat on either side of him in the backseat.

The police got into their cars and led us back to the pier with forty minutes to spare before we departed. I accompanied the ensign to the quarter deck of the *Hale* and turned him over to their operations officer.

We returned to the *Abbot*, checked in our weapons, and prepared to go to sea. The captain later congratulated me. J.J. and Ski also were told later individually by the captain that he was very pleased at how well they had done.

I never did get to see Sophia perform, but what I did see of her at her apartment, plus the state of the "errant ensign," left no doubt about her entrancing charms.

Chapter 20

Father of the Bride—The Bliss of Being Relieved of Responsibilities

June 14, 2014, loomed large on the horizon. Our daughter was about to marry a great guy named Bill McKeever. It was a first marriage for both of them, though they had both rounded the forty-year mark. But who am I to criticize? I'm no spring chicken either.

It was a week away from the day I had been waiting for since Jenny was born. I was so arthritic and overweight that I wasn't sure I could make it down the aisle with her. Just the thought of it exhausted me and, if that wasn't enough, our little house in Essex, CT, had become the command center for all of the activities leading up to "D-Day."

FedEx trucks dropped things off and picked things up several times a day; the phones rang incessantly; cars deposited family and friends from far-flung places like Texas, California, Canada, Denmark, and the like to lend a hand.

Naturally, as the father, I assumed that I was in command of the chaos. A wise man once said that "assumption is the mother of confusion." I got the message before the main event began.

As the out-of-town family and guests began to arrive, my observations and well-meaning suggestions began to fall on more and more deaf ears. I became increasingly irrelevant and was hardly missed as my trips to the Black Seal, my favorite watering hole, and frequent naps mounted in length and number.

I soon realized that I was no longer in control and, more importantly, I no longer wanted to be. This was an incredible milestone for me, who has been lovingly referred to by my family over the years as the Supreme Commander, the Enforcer, Napoleon, and worse!

On the first day of the "morning meeting" to discuss the wedding preparations, my attempt to hijack the gathering was repelled, and I retreated to my office and ate my breakfast on a tray with the door closed, following orders to focus on my assignment of the day: to open the late replies to the wedding invitations and maintain an accurate count of acceptances and declines.

I wasn't the only one in the line of fire. Jenny's dog Ladybug soon scratched at the door. I let her in. She too was also "underfoot." Apparently she could not fit under our bed with the cat, who had been in hiding for several days.

Was this my house, or some third-world sweatshop? One afternoon in the living room, Ladybug was fitted for a dress for her part in the ceremony (the image of a fat black lab desperately trying to wriggle her way out of a cloud of pink and white taffeta will be forever burned into my mind), while other willing hands, including grandchildren, were on the outside deck spooning birdseed into little satin sacks tied with bows for the wedding guests to pelt the newlyweds with as they exited the church.

The next day the group was assigned to fill twenty cardboard boxes with the makings of the table centerpieces, which included ship models and dozens of small apothecary bottles to be filled with white roses and calla lilies at the wedding tent on the morning of the reception.

After three days of this stuff, I just wanted it all to be over. Thank God for my den and its thick, soundproof door; for my new best friend and fellow cellmate, Ladybug; and for the Black Seal to retreat to!

When I tried to resign completely from the tasks at hand, I was told by my wife and daughter curtly, "Resignation accepted." However, I was dutifully informed that I still had two jobs to do, and these were non-negotiable: to walk Jenny down the aisle and to sing a duet with Bill.

The big day finally arrived. I had practiced the walk up and down the aisle (making a guest appearance at our local church for the first time since the previous Christmas) and had every confidence that I could make it as far as the altar, although my aching legs were not so sure.

In a weak moment a month before the wedding, my future son-in-law Bill had convinced me to sing a duet with him to our wives at the reception. Four stanzas of "If Ever I Would Leave You" from the Broadway show *Camelot*. I practiced and practiced. I sang in the shower. I sang in the pool every day as I exercised.

Compounding the fact that I can't carry a note with a wheelbarrow, I could not for the life of me memorize just two of the four short stanzas I was supposed to sing, but I must admit that with the shower door closed, my voice was beginning to sound better and better!

D-Day, June 14, 2014. Reveille 5:30 a.m. I eased out of bed, groggy from the rehearsal festivities and the drinks at the Griswold Inn the evening before. The rest of the house was still fast asleep. I made a pot of coffee, poured a cup, tiptoed out to the car, and headed downtown to buy the morning papers. I drove to the foot of Main Street and watched the sun rising to reflect off the white hulls of the boats moored offshore. Then I drove to the Essex Yacht Club to check on the tent for the reception.

The town was empty, the yacht club quiet, and the weather still and perfect. The location of the tent with its view of the moored boats was classic. All the chaos of the previous week faded as I drove back. But by the time I arrived back at the house, pandemonium had broken loose again. Apparently, my wife was supposed to be picking up the flowers, but I had escaped with the only car big enough to fit the many bouquets and arrangements. Everyone had spent the last thirty minutes calling all over town. "Have you seen a white SUV drive by?" It sounded like a reprisal of the O.J. Simpson chase!

Dorothy and Jenny gave me a serious dressing-down. Couldn't I do anything right? Chastened and contrite, I left with Dorothy to rush off and retrieve the flowers. By the time we got to the yacht club, family members and friends were busy arranging the table centerpieces under Jenny's direction.

I got dressed very early to clear the way for the ladies. At 4:00 p.m., our neighbor Ralph arrived in the driveway behind the wheel of a vintage Rolls-Royce that would take Jenny and me to the church.

Ralph walked Jenny from the house to the opened door of the door of the Rolls, as family friend and ace photographer Ken Paprocki snapped away. She was stunning in a full-length, champagne-colored, pure silk crepe gown with a plunging backline and crystal-sequined bodice, last worn by my mother to a U.S. Embassy dance in London in 1927.

We arrived a little late at the church. The wedding party was milling around in the vestibule. As the first notes of the processional music sounded, my stomach suddenly turned into knots.

Jenny and I were alone now in the vestibule when we heard the first notes of "Here Comes the Bride." The verger opened the doors, but one got jammed. As Jenny and I both tried to enter at the same time, we got stuck in the doorway. I turned sideways and catapulted Jenny headfirst into the church. She managed to keep her balance and grip on her bouquet. As we neared the altar, I remarked to Jenny that Bill and his groomsmen looked like a police line-up on a Saturday night. She laughed out loud as I handed her off to Bill. My first assignment was completed successfully!

The second task I had been dreading came midway through the reception. Alex Donner, the amazingly talented orchestra leader, called Bill and me to the bandstand. First, Bill sang a flawless, Sinatra-like version of "Strangers in the Night" to Jenny. Then Alex handed me a microphone, and I promptly forgot all of the words to the song Bill and I were supposed to sing together. Fortunately, Alex had an iPod that displayed the words in large capital letters. At the end of our duet, with the crowd cheering, Bill leaned over and yelled to me, "We're going to Vegas!"

My part in the wedding, though small in the overall planning and preparation, had changed from that of a bit player to a starring role in several key cameo appearances. I was important after all!

I used to be a big shot with a team of people reporting to me at work and a wife and family who actually listened to me. At eighty-two, I've resigned myself to the fact that I no longer wield such power. My triumphs now are minor victories. I figured out how to turn on the microwave! I finished the daily Sudoku game in *The New York Post*! But I'm okay with that. With less power comes less responsibility. And, frankly, it's nice to while away the days as I want, happily tapping away on my laptop, floating belly and toes up in the pool, blarneying my way to a free round at the Black Seal, and spending an afternoon snoozing with cat on the bed and dog at my feet whenever I damn well please.

After the wedding, Jenny and Bill flew off for a multi-week honeymoon in Italy and Greece. They called us to check in from time to time. It may be good to be young and full of energy. But, hot damn, it's also pretty great to be old, at home, with the remote control in hand, heading off to a long, lazy nap with no alarm clock in sight.

Chapter 21

Love Above All—A Future Get-Out-of-Jail Card for My Grandchildren

Richard Haskel is more than a friend, he's like a brother—he always has your back. To no one's surprise, he married a lovely woman and raised a great family. Over the years, Dorothy and I and our two kids have joined Richard and Jane and their two children, Trish and Whit, for vacations on Fire Island, in Salisbury, Connecticut, and even at the 1980 Lake Placid Olympics. On more than one occasion, Richard and I were forced to play bad cops and confiscate carefully hidden cases of beer or bottles of vodka from our offspring, pretending we were shocked and horrified by their antics.

In the event that I am incapacitated—or run off screaming to a desert island—when my grandchildren and Richard's hit their late teens, I am leaving behind this story as a gift to them. They are to use it to prove to their parents that they should not be held responsible for any errant ways that were handed down to them through their DNA on their granddad's side.

I was comfortably ensconced on the third floor of Lawrence, the dusty brick dorm near the main gateway to the freshman campus at Yale. It was September 1951. Two large bedrooms, each with a desk and double-decker bunks and a high-ceilinged living room, would be my home for my first year at college.

My three roommates and I were cocky and exhibited this to varying degrees. We were a collection of jocks with one world-class singer in our ranks. The world was our oyster!

One early March morning about 2:00 a.m., the phone rang and rang. I finally got up and stumbled into the living room to pick it up.

"Rider, this is Burns. I'm in jail."

"What? Where?"

"I only get one call. I need $75 or I'm in here for life. Here are the directions. Hurry!" Click.

John Burns's roommates hadn't bothered to pick up their phone. At that stage of our lives, coming up with $75 was like floating a bond issue, particularly in the middle of the night. I had six singles and a dollar in change. My roommates and Burns's contributed $32. We fanned out, banging on doors until our take totaled $85; the overage would cover gas and tolls. Another buddy named Thorne volunteered to drive. Forty-five minutes later, we pulled into the state troopers' barracks in Meriden, anxious to hear Burns's story firsthand.

The desk sergeant dispelled our curiosity. He gave an outline of our friend's transgressions. Caught up in the moment,

Burns decided to commemorate a particularly gratifying evening he'd had with a gal pal from Smith College. On the way home from North Hampton and just off the Wilbur Cross Highway, he remembered an old factory building he had passed many times. The building housed the Burns Tire and Rubber Company. Prominently displayed on the roof of the three-story warehouse was a sign bearing his name (no relation), emblazoned in neon lights, which read Burns Satisfies.

Burns had pulled off the highway and into the parking lot. He had to have that sign. Armed with the wrench used to change a flat and fueled with requited desire and a taste of John Barleycorn, he clambered up the fire escape ladder to the roof and "liberated" the sign bearing his name.

So far, so good! Now came the hard part. The sign was too long to fit in the car, so Burns's higher education kicked in. He rolled down both back windows and placed the sign crosswise over the backseat with the ends of the sign extending out on either side of the car.

The problem occurred at the tollgate. The car wouldn't fit through. The toll collector notified the troopers. On top of all this, Burns was driving without a license, and there was the smell of several beers on his breath.

By the time the trooper had finished the tale for us, Burns was produced from his cell, none the worse for wear. After he was properly receipted, we hastily departed. On the way home, he related his version of the story. It didn't vary too much from that of the trooper's although, of course, the details were more specific and the language more colorful.

Burns still had one more hurdle to overcome. The car that had carried him to Smith was not his. He had borrowed it from his friend Richard Haskel, a freshman football teammate.

To complicate matters even further, the car wasn't Richard's either. It belonged to Richard's brother Merwin, who was an upperclassman. Freshmen were not allowed to have cars. Richard had borrowed it from Merwin with specific instructions that no one else was to get behind the wheel. Burns had badgered Richard until he finally gave in.

The night of Burns's adventure, Richard was sound asleep in his bed. He arose early, turned on the radio, and tuned in to the news while still half asleep. The newscaster was relating the story of a Yale freshman named Burns, detailing that "the sign that wouldn't fit through the tollgate." Suddenly Richard was wide awake. His first reaction was, "What the hell am I going to tell Merwin?"

Merwin was home in Scarsdale, recuperating from a bout of mononucleosis. He had missed a whole term and, fortunately for Richard, would not return to school until after spring break.

The only part of the story to occur without incident took place the following day. Thorne drove Richard to Meridan to retrieve Merwin's car. Burns was conspicuously absent. Merwin would not learn of the saga until well after spring break, and when he did, there was hell to pay. Burns may have satisfied some—but certainly not Merwin!

Chapter 22

The Power of Kindness— Surviving Life's Great Losses

I have so many fond memories of my childhood, in particular my time at Andover. One of the main reasons is that I got to share that experience with my only sibling, my younger brother Ken.

More than a half-century later, I was invited to attend what would have been his fiftieth reunion at Andover and its sister school Abbot. The Sunday memorial service in Cochran Chapel would honor absent friends or classmates who had passed on. As each name was read, a relative or classmate walked up the aisle and placed a ribbon in a special box. The interval allowed us a moment to reflect on happy times and shared events of long ago.

I had helped run my own fiftieth reunion the year before before. I looked forward to attending Ken's, but with the anticipation also came waves of dread. My first wife, Betsy Waskowitz, attended Abbot and graduated the same year as Ken. She died of lymphatic cancer on November 14, 1963, at age twenty-nine, leaving me shattered and alone. In 1995, at age sixty-one, my brother Ken died suddenly of an undetected heart condition. Two of the most important people in my life had gone much too soon. The memorial service that weekend would honor both, bringing back cherished memories but also searing pain.

Seated ten pews back on the right side of the chapel, I clutched one of two ribbons I was given, waiting for Betsy's name to be called. Then came the flashbacks. Friday evening calling hours. Our cozy home in New Canaan, Connecticut. Betsy's prize-winning painting hanging in Brace Hall on the Abbot Campus. Her early battle with polio, and her tenacious fifteen-month fight against cancer. When I heard her name called, I was on my feet. I placed the ribbon in the box and returned to my seat, more than a little shaken.

Now it was time for the boys. I held the remaining ribbon and again came the flashbacks, this time of Ken. Christmases with Mom and Dad. Endless summers lifeguarding together on Fire Island. Playing hockey and lacrosse together. Trudging alongside each other in a blinding snowstorm. Serving together as officers on the USS *Abbot*.

After the service, I walked down the long aisle toward the vestibule, alone with my memories, rapt in the moment, oblivious to the crowd. My thoughts shifted to my adored wife, Dorothy, our daughter Jenny, son Graham and his wife Paulette, and our grandchildren, Graham Jr., Bradley, Victoria, and Duncan. How fortunate I was.

Suddenly in the back of the church I saw the head of school, a wonderful woman named Barbara Landis Chase. Without a word, she walked towards me, smiled knowingly, and hugged me. I always will cherish her heartfelt hug and thoughtfulness.

The pain of losing a loved one never goes away. It's stored down deep inside. Hit the nerve or cross the tripwire and the emotions come storming back. But the death of a friend or a family member can sometimes be easier to deal with when you get older. You're more willing to accept hugs and support. There's no more need to pretend you're macho. You can also couch all those you've lost with all of the other memories and people you've accrued since they left you. To go on, to endure, is to honor the people you've loved and lost. It's what they would have wanted. If the situation were reversed, it's surely what you would have wanted for them.

Chapter 23

Murphy's Law—
When the World Feels
Overwhelming

With the horrible winter of 2014 finally in the rear-view mirror, this next tale may make me sound like a grumpy old poop. (Dorothy would say, "But, George, you are a grumpy old poop!") This story illustrates the meaning of Murphy's Law. If anything can go wrong, it will—especially when you hit old age.

It began the day before Christmas Eve in 2013 and continued until mid-March of 2014.

"Dear, I'm going to have a gin and tonic. How about you?" I asked my beloved around 5:00 p.m. on December 23.

"Great, just leave the lime and the tonic out and I'll make mine a little later," she replied.

I opened the freezer section of the refrigerator to find chocolate ice cream leaking into the ice cube bin. Obviously, the fridge had died, and this was a problem because it was bulging with food for the holiday festivities.

We salvaged some of the contents, but the milk and most of the perishables had to be thrown out. We bought a new fridge the next morning, but had to wait until it was delivered. Meanwhile, Christmas dinner was moved next door to our son and daughter-in-law's house, and a new turkey and all the trimmings were purchased.

When the new fridge finally arrived, it didn't fit. Dorothy and I were irate. "But we gave you the measurements!" I hollered into the phone at the appliance salesman.

"Just a minute, sir," said a flat, distant voice on the other end of the receiver. He came back on the line and read me the dimensions—so many inches across, so many down, and so many deep.

"Wait a minute," I dug in, "That's not right. That can't be what I told you!" They were off by several inches.

"Sir, I have what you told us right here—*in your handwriting.*"

"Yikes." I hung up and related the call to Dorothy.

"George, you're not getting any younger. You have to take your time and be careful when you do things."

"That's it. I'm going to the Seal!" I stormed off in search of my favorite bar stool.

When I returned home contrite, Dorothy and I premeasured the alcove where the fridge was to sit. With her help, we took our time, were extra careful, and got the measurements right. (The only thing worse than getting older and less competent is having a wife who is also getting older but somehow better and smarter!) We called the appliance store, and they arranged to come by to make the new fridge fit.

Life resumed at its normal pace after the holidays. But on February 4, I woke up at 5:30 a.m. to find the house as cold as a mausoleum. The furnace was as dead as our fridge had been six weeks before. (In fact, it was so cold inside, we didn't even need a fridge anymore!)

"Dear, you check the oil gauge in the basement. I'll get these bozos on the phone!" I instructed my wife.

It wasn't my first run-in with this oil company. To compound matters, the automated answering inquisition, "Press 1 for English . . . This call may be recorded . . . if you know your party's extension . . ." took five minutes of my precious time. I was finally transferred to Steve in the service department. Service, my ass! The line had so much static on it, I could barely hear him.

"Where are you?" I bellowed.

"New Delhi."

Just then, my daughter Jenny, home for a visit, swept into my office. "What's wrong?" she mouthed.

"Can't hear a goddamned thing!"

In one lightning-fast move, she played with the buttons on the phone and—presto—I could hear the service guy's voice, clear as a bell.

"Dad, you either have to learn how to use the volume control on that phone or you need to get a hearing aid!" She waltzed off in disgust.

I resumed my focus on the task at hand, but my mood further darkened when Steve told me he would book a service call three days hence. "We're out of oil, god damn it!" I yelled into the phone. "It may be warm where you are, but it's twelve degrees outside and forty-one here in the house. Hear that noise? That's the sound of my dog's teeth chattering! I'll be eighty-two in May and my wife turns eighty next month. We've made it this far. I'm not going to let us freeze to death waiting for you ding-dongs to get around to us. Put someone on the phone who can help us *now*!"

Just before noon, a repairman arrived and determined that the problem was not the furnace; it was the fuel gauge that was faulty. The cause was a malfunctioning jet pump in our well that supplies water pressure to the circulation system. The pressure was too low to start the furnace and heat the boiler. The pump was buried under a foot and a half of now hard-packed snow, left over from the latest storm, five feet below the frozen tundra.

The first night without heat, Dorothy and I awoke to bone-chilling cold. The weather turned uglier, and the temperature stayed well below freezing, even diving to zero one night. Our plumber hired a landscaper with a backhoe and purchased a new jet pump assembly. The weather broke enough in mid-February to allow the workers to locate the well and dig down to replace the pump. Finally, thank God, after a week of freezing our toes off, we were once again on our way to having heat!

Our joy was short-lived, however, when later that same day, Dorothy discovered water in the basement. The oil company was called again, and the workman returned and isolated what they thought was the source of the leak—an errant air conditioner unit, located in a crawl space in the basement, accessible only by a wooden door, which couldn't be opened (of course). Our plumber arrived soon thereafter and cut off all water in the house to confirm the exact source and cause of the gushing water. At one point, we had seven different workers coming and going up and down the cellar stairs off of our dining room. I was stationed at my command post at the head of the table. Marybeth and Ladybug retreated to the cold bedroom in all the confusion.

Luckily our age and its attendant bouts of anxiety and worst-case-scenario thinking had prompted Dorothy and myself (well, okay, Dorothy) to fill both bathtubs with water prior to the storm. We thanked heavens for the supply, which we now had to use to flush the toilets. The bucket brigade began in earnest. Luckily, Dorothy had also stockpiled plenty of bottled water and bags of ice cubes.

Between the fireplace, the den, and the propane heated stove, we survived eight long nights at "Camp Run-a-Muck." Each evening our cat joined us in bed, with Jenny's dog taking up room on the floor at our feet, making any movement—including oft-required trips to the bathroom—perilous in the dead of the night.

The entire series of disasters unfolded over more than two weeks, from the first discovery that there was no water pressure coming out of the taps and no heat, to the diagnosis of the problem, to the cleaning up and drying out, to the grand finale. What an unholy mess. The heat finally came back on in stages, allowing us to return to our bedroom.

For eight days and eight nights at the height of February's winter fury, Dorothy and I huddled in our home. It made us appreciate the little things in life: warmth, johns that flush, showers and tubs with warm water, shaving in the bathroom sink, not in the kitchen over a bowl of water warmed from the stove.

We got through it with our marriage and senses of humor intact (barely). Why is it that mishaps seem so much more overwhelming when you get older? When I asked my daughter this, she gave me a hug then said, "At least you're here for them to happen to, and at least you have your children (or "staff") around to help you."

"You're right, I suppose," I said and grabbed another tissue. The whole episode led to a four-way cold shared by Dorothy, myself, the cat, and the dog. But I can't help but believe Mr. Murphy exerts his law disproportionately at us old-timers. How else can you explain how things can get so complicated?

Chapter 24

Dad and the Pewter Tankard—Paying Homage to a Parent

It was a quiet Saturday afternoon in August, and Dorothy and I were enjoying a lazy weekend at home. The weather was near perfect: warm, sunny, and a nearly cloudless sky with low humidity. Lately our routine in the afternoons was to mix a gin and tonic and go for a swim. Today was no different.

I like to get my exercise by walking in the shallow end of our pool, but walking can be boring. Sometimes I sing show tunes way off-key or think of things to write about or just look at the woods and sky and remember. Dorothy usually sits at our poolside table and reads, with Jenny's lab Ladybug sitting next to her.

We mix our drinks in pewter tankards that my father bought on his last trip from England on the *Queen Elizabeth 2*. Before entering the water, I place mine on the side of the pool and periodically I stop my exercising for a sip. When I looked at the tankard, my eyes focused on the small Queen Elizabeth crest on its side.

Dad had died at age eighty-six on February 2, 1986. He was a Brit and served in World War I. His corvette vessel was torpedoed off Ireland. The German U-boat surfaced and machine-gunned the survivors. He was one of a handful to live, though he was grazed by a bullet in the back of his scalp and wounded in the right knee. He loved the sea and was hired as a radio officer by the Cunard White Star Lines and then became a cruise director. In his later years, his service earned him a yearly roundtrip passage to England.

After Mother died in June 1978, Dad traveled every year to England to visit his brother, two sisters, and my cousin Nora. As he aged, the trip became more difficult. He insisted on going and stubbornly resisted our entreaties about getting a helper aboard.

I drove Dad to Pier Ninety the day he sailed in September 1985, the last trip of his life. After I parked the car, I walked him to the embarkation checkpoint with his bags and helped check him in. He was carrying a briefcase and a double thermos carrier with a handle. The thermos bottles had been replaced by two quarts of Dewar's Scotch. Dad was frail; his military posture and rapid gait were now gone. His shuffle made me think we should not let him go at all.

Dad would never take any money from us, even though he was of limited means in his later years. We were able, however, to convince him to sell his house and move with his dog and cat to a lovely suite we built for him in a converted garage. When I shook his hand and gave him a hug, I handed him an envelope and asked him to read what was in it later at sea. I watched him as he made his way slowly down the pier to the gangway. He turned and waved.

The night before, I had written a note from us assuring him that we would take good care of his lab and his cat. I also included four one-hundred-dollar bills.

I left the pier and had no stomach for going to work, so I called the office and told them that I had a late lunch downtown and probably wouldn't be back. Instead I drove to the World Trade Center, parked my car, and took an elevator to the Windows on the World restaurant. I got a window-side table with an unobstructed view of the Hudson. I ordered a drink and settled in to wait for the *QE2* to go by. My thoughts turned to Dad on board the ship. Knowing Cunard, I felt secure in the knowledge that once he unpacked, he would be hovered over at every turn. There was no way we could have stopped him from going and, if the worst happened, he would be at peace either at sea or with his beloved family in England.

I snapped out of my reverie. Two tug boats appeared as I looked up the Hudson. I watched as the *QE2* came sailing past. When she came abeam, I raised my glass to Dad, shed a tear, and kept my gaze steady until the stern all but disappeared on her way to the Atlantic.

Dad called us several times to let us know about his visits with relatives and old friends. He was managing quite well but returned somewhat weary in mid-October. It seemed that he knew this would be his last trip. He was happy to be home but sadly reflective of what had become of his beloved England. He lamented the social changes that had taken place, which seemed to have altered the spirit of the proud and powerful country for which he had fought. He forecast correctly that the U.S. and Canada would shortly follow the same path.

Christmas came, and Dad perked up when our kids came home from school. Dad's gifts to me that Christmas were the four *QE2* pewter tankards.

After Christmas, Dad started getting weaker. The world, his world, was changing and there was nothing he could do about it. He spent a lot of time watching the news and going over his papers. On January 28, Dad, like so many of us, watched the launch of the Space Shuttle *Challenger* and its subsequent destruction. It distressed him deeply, particularly the death of Christa McAuliffe, the New Hampshire high school history teacher, wife, and mother of two children.

A few days later, Graham's hockey team came down from Boston to play St. John's in back-to-back games on Long Island. Graham was captain, and he got permission to stay with us the night before with two of his teammates. They won their first game, and Dad was going to come with us to the second game, but decided to stay home and grill steaks for us afterwards. He walked Graham and his two teammates over to the waiting car for their trip to the rink. One of the boys said later that Dad had tears in his eyes when he hugged Graham goodbye.

It was just getting dark when we arrived home from the game. Dorothy and Jenny got out and walked past Dad's garage apartment. Dorothy looked through the window and saw him lying on his bed at an awkward angle, staring up toward the ceiling. She yelled to me and we went in. Lester Lanin's big band music was playing on the phonograph. The dog was wagging his tail, standing at the foot of the bed, and the cat was by Dad's side.

On the nightstand there was a half-empty glass of Scotch and water. Dad must have gone to heaven moments before we returned. There were still ice cubes in the glass. I called his doctor, who was also Dad's close friend and neighbor. He determined that the inoperable abdominal aortic aneurysm that had been discovered five years before had finally burst.

Thirty years later, I was looking at the pewter tankard Dad had given me the Christmas before he died. It gives me some consolation to know that he went quickly and peacefully with his animals by his side and his favorite music playing. Not a day goes by that I don't think about him and all that he meant to me. I hope my kids will feel the same when it's my time.

Chapter 25

Mouthing Off—Don't Shoot From the Lip

I've always had a big mouth and a quick temper and that sometimes gets me in trouble. What can I say? I'm fightin' Irish with a bit of Scot and Brit mixed in. Despite my family's hopes, age has not mellowed me. In fact, I've found—as you may have too—that age seems to draw out and magnify my flaws. Oh well!

However, I've also discovered (rather happily) that as I've grown older, I don't really care that damned much anymore. "I'm me," I tell my wife and kids, as though that's an excusable line of defense.

Perhaps it's because I am near deaf and refuse to get a hearing aid (stubbornness is another one of my operating flaws), but I just don't think screaming at the TV or the jerk who beeps his horn at me just because I may have nodded off at a stoplight turning green, is such a terrible vice. The way I think about it is that screaming involves deep breathing, so it must be aerobic and burn calories. When I'm really pissed and jumping up and down, I figure it must be exercise!

When I try to make this case to Dorothy, she shakes her head and walks away. Then I know I'm really in trouble. To help get me back on the right track and back into her good graces, I like to remember other times in my shady past when mouthing off led to big problems. Somehow, reliving those "Oh, sh**!" moments helps me to focus and shape up!

One such moment occurred back in 1955. I had reported aboard the USS *Preston* (DD-795) which was a Fletcher-class destroyer, home ported in Newport, Rhode Island. After graduating from college the month before, my preparation had been weekly NROTC classes and a five-week midshipman cruise during the previous summer.

It was the Fourth of July weekend, and Newport was buzzing with summer revelers and sailors. Shops were crowded, and the bars were busy on Thames Street. I got off the bus from Providence at Ships Landing. The *Preston* was moored out in the harbor, with three other destroyers abreast of it.

The post-WWII peace was playing out while the major political forces were still jockeying for position. Though the summer of 1955 was a period of relative calm, tensions were elevating in the Middle East and on the continent.

My father had been injured in the war during his time in the British Navy. He knew that despite the romance and excitement of what lay ahead for me, "All might not be beer and Skittles."

I eagerly boarded the fifty-foot liberty launch with my duffle bag and suitcase in hand. When we approached the *Preston*, I scrambled up the steps to the waiting office of the deck. I made a quick salute to the flag on the stern and then another to the OOD.

"Permission to come aboard, sir."

"Permission granted."

I was shown into the wardroom by the OOD, who was also an ensign or junior officer like myself.

Ensigns are assigned to major departments aboard ship like Gunnery or Engineering. In my case, I was assigned to the Deck Department on the Gunnery. This consisted of two divisions with approximately twenty men each, headed by first class boatswain's mates who reported to a chief petty officer, who reported to me. In addition to my responsibilities in the Gunnery Department and as Division Officer, my collateral duties included positions as Athletics Officer, Small Boat Officer, Torpedo Officer, and Assistant Anti-Submarine Warfare Officer. I was also Welfare and Recreation Officer (they certainly picked the right guy for the latter). It sounds like a lot of work, but few of the collateral duties overlapped time-wise. The deck divisions are responsible for hull maintenance such as chipping and painting, refueling at sea, tying up and mooring the ship, standing deck watches at sea and in port, and training all new sailors when they come on board, many of whom transfer to other divisions depending on need, aptitude, and skills.

Our first operation was a HUK (hunter-killer) exercise pitting a surface ship convoy against a pack of prowling submarines conducted in the North Atlantic. The convoy consisted of a carrier, supply ships, and two tankers, protected by a screen of destroyers and destroyer escorts. This was a combined effort including ships and subs from the U.S. Navy, the British Navy, and the Canadian Navy.

For four days we played cat and mouse with the subs. I was standing watches in the sonar room and on the bridge, trying to my mind my Ps and Qs and be a model of decorum. On the second day, our position on the radar screen was about 4:30 on a clock dial. Sonar picked up a contact. The operator locked on to the sub, and we prepared to engage. The OOD ordered course and speed changes to intercept the sub and "sink" it. The hedgehog mounts and the depth-charge racks carrying weapons were manned and ready. I was on the bridge, standing watch as Junior OOD. The starboard lookout shouted, "Torpedo wake amidships!" to starboard while his binoculars were fixed on the bubbly white trail left as the torpedo streaked towards us.

The captain took command, "I have the con. All ahead flank, hard right rudder, come to course 285." The white path passed just astern of us. The captain ordered course and speed changes to continue the attack. Sonar was still locked on the sub.

We made our pass. To simulate the actual attack on the sub, a percussion grenade was dropped at the proper moment. The chief, who was standing on the stern, pulled the firing pin and lobbed the grenade overboard. It exploded "harmlessly" close to the sub.

We were credited with a kill. "Yes!" I bellowed and held my arms up high in victory, then quickly scrambled to recover my composure.

We were designated to retrieve the torpedo and return it to the sub. Our twenty-six-foot whaleboat was rigged outboard, suspended from davits on the port side of the ship, and positioned at deck level for quick access, in preparation for the retrieval. The crew consisted of the chief boatswain, a coxswain, an engineer, and two sailors.

The bright orange tip of the torpedo, bobbing up and down in the heavy swells, was spotted by the seaman in the bow, about a thousand yards downwind.

The bow-hook sailor snared the notched tip of the torpedo with a boat hook and steadied it by passing a line through the hole in the nose, and then secured the line to the bow post.

As we increased speed, the back of the torpedo rose parallel to our boat, making it easier to secure to our portside.

The sub had surfaced about a mile south of us. As we neared, three officers on the conning tower and the swarm of sailors on deck were readying for our arrival. Through a bullhorn we heard, "Make your approach."

The cox made a near-perfect landing. Just as we were about to untie the torpedo, an officer on the deck of the sub waved us off.

We were so close aboard that the heaving of our boat in a large swell caused the torpedo to wedge between us and the "bubble" of the sub and tilt the whaleboat severely outboard. We shipped a lot of water. The torpedo was still firmly secured to us fore and aft.

"Let's get out of here!" I hollered.

The cox pushed the tiller hard toward the sub and a wave lifted us free from the "bubble." As we moved away, I screamed up at the conning tower, "The next time you assholes wave us in, be ready!"

Our second attempt got the job done, but I was still pissed. We had experienced a near-miss.

Our captain wanted to know why it had taken two tries to return the torpedo. He had watched the whole thing through binoculars from his chair on the starboard wing of the bridge. I filled him in and omitted my intemperate outburst. He complimented me and asked me to pass on his congratulations to the crew.

Several days later the exercises were complete. All the ships entered Halifax Harbor for several days of liberty. The Canadians were incredible hosts. In addition to the usual bus tours, walking tours, lectures, and shopping, a number of special events were planned. Our ship won a two-day softball tournament held at Dalhousie University.

The first night ashore, our wardroom was invited to a reception aboard one of the British destroyers. The senior officers had exited early. Our junior officer challenged the

Brits to a rugby match in their wardroom. Two bloody noses and a lot of lager later, all of us left together to sample the exciting nightlife of downtown Halifax.

The last night dinner-dance was a more formal affair. Each ship's officers were seated together at assigned tables. Busloads of pretty Canadian maritime ladies joined us for cocktails and a grand buffet. There was also a great band for dancing.

Suddenly I felt a tap on my shoulder. I spun around and there before me was a smiling lieutenant with dolphins pinned to his chest. "Red, do you have a second? There's someone who would like a word with you."

The memory of cussing out the officers on the sub's conning tower appeared before. My initial reaction was, "My God, I've done it again!"

"Please come with me," the lieutenant said curtly.

I was led to a long table on the other side of the dance floor. As we approached, the commander rose to greet us.

"Have a seat, Red. I'm the skipper of the sub you engaged. I know your name as Ensign George Rider. I'm one of the assholes you yelled at."

All eyes at the table were on me. The sub's captain and I were still standing. He towered over me.

"I met your Captain at an operation briefing this afternoon. I told him that his boat did a great job in choppy waters retrieving my fish. Sit down and have a drink with us, and, by the way, a word of advice: The next time you feel compelled to call senior officers assholes, keep your cap on. Your red hair is a dead giveaway!"

So, I guess you'd say the moral of the story is, loose lips not only sink ships; they can also sink ensigns!

Chapter 26

St. Patrick's Eve Tragedy—Telling the Stories of Heroes

Some stories buried in time cry out to be told. The St. Patrick's Eve Tragedy of 1956 is one of them. One of the great joys of taking up writing as my passion in retirement is to tell the stories of those who valiantly put others' lives before their own—and often paid the ultimate price.

In late October 2007, my daughter Jenny and I were attending an alumni meeting at the school we both attended. After dinner she arrived at my table with a young man in tow. "Dad," she said, "meet Harry Flynn. I think you were in the Navy with his dad."

Indeed I was. We were roommates aboard the USS *Preston* in 1955. I had not spoken with Harry Sr. in fifty-two years. The next morning, Harry Jr. called his father and handed me the phone.

As a result of that chance encounter, Harry Sr. and I began to swap stories. One of his in particular caught my attention. It was his retelling of the harrowing events of St. Patrick's Eve in 1956 in Newport Harbor, Rhode Island, to which I had my own personal connection.

Ironically, another chance encounter at the 19th Hole Bar of Southward Ho, our local country club on Long Island, also turned to that same ill-fated day. Doc Petit, a neighbor, had also been home ported in Newport. Doc, then a medical corpsman aboard the destroyer tender *Cascade*, had also witnessed the same terrifying events.

Their stories triggered my own memories. I thought about how two old friends from different phases of my life had both been there at the scene of the tragedy, how I had almost been there with them, and why all three of us had been spared while our fellow shipmates hadn't been nearly as lucky. I spent days researching what happened by tracking down long forgotten newspaper articles from the Newport library and piecing together the following events.

St. Patrick's Day has come to be known for parades, parties, and celebration. For four brave Navy men, what happened in 1956 was just the opposite. My friend Harry had been attached to the commodore's staff headquartered on the USS *Irwin*, which was temporarily based in Newport. That night, Harry had the staff watch. "A lot of people had already left the ship on liberty," he recalled. "We were nested together, four Fletcher-class destroyers, twenty-one hundred tons of seagoing greyhounds. I was waiting for my fiancée and her cousin to visit for supper by launch and then return and drive back to Boston. We had arrived from the Charleston Navy Shipyard in Boston after our overhaul. A ship just out of the yard is always in a state of flux. New people and old hands are getting familiar with or reviewing their duties. This time, everything worked against us." Adding to the problem, a number of senior officers were not aboard the ships at that time, leaving their junior counterparts in charge.

Harry said that the ship's crew could tell a storm was coming, but storms in Newport in February weren't exactly headline news. As they rounded Nantucket Light on the trip from Boston, the hatch above Harry's bunk sprung open and water from the bow flooded the sleeping area. He leapt up and headed topside.

The Newport storm came up quickly and violently. The winds howled and snow turned into a blizzard with seventy-mile-per-hour winds overnight.

"Storms aren't unusual," Harry told me, "but they're never fun. We sent the liberty launch in at 4:00 p.m. (1600 hours). The wind had come up and the trip was very rough. When the boat crew returned for another trip, the forty-foot launch landed between the sterns of the *Preston* and the *Irwin*. I went to the commodore, my boss, and suggested he decide when to cease boating. It was getting very rough out there. He said to stop them after the next boat returns. I went to the stern of the *Irwin* where the launch was tying up."

Meanwhile, crewman Kenneth R. Kane, fireman rate (or rank) from New York City, was part of the crew manning the forty-foot motor launch that was being moved to a more sheltered position, moored to a buoy behind the nest of four destroyers. A gust of wind ripped through the air, tossing the launch so high on the waves that its keel could be seen from the destroyer deck.

As the launch neared the USS *Preston*, two of the boat crew jumped across to board the destroyer. When Kane tried to follow, he fell into the freezing water. The men aboard the ship yelled to throw him a line, but a rope could not be found. Suddenly, the launch heaved high on another huge wave and crashed down on Kane, likely breaking his back. Crewmen from the *Preston* scrambled down and grabbed Kane by his life jacket, but he was torn from their grasp when a strap broke. He slipped through the jacket and disappeared into the churning water, leaving the sailors holding the empty jacket. The motor launch drifted away.

Officers aboard the *Preston* quickly ordered out a whale-boat with five brave men aboard to aid in the rescue. Two of them, Lieutenant Junior Grade Juergens and Reese B. Kingsmore, boarded the motor launch, restarted its engine, and returned to the *Preston*.

The others—Moore, Britton, and Hutchinson—stayed in the whaleboat and kept up a vain search for the missing Kane. Moore served as coxswain, although that was not his normal duty. Before he left the *Preston*, he told shipmates he was going along "to make sure everything went right."

As Harry recalled, "The men set out into the now-swirling snow. The wind had come up with a wild ferocity and the heavy snowfall limited vision to a few feet from the nest. I reported back to the commodore, who wanted me to stay on the situation and report to him. There wasn't much to report for some time. I stayed in the wardroom, with an ensign I didn't know too well and his girlfriend aboard for a visit. The storm was wicked that night and we were constantly worrying about the nest breaking up or drifting."

Tragically, Harry was right to worry. Doc Petit, also in the harbor that night, witnessed the second, somber part of the story: "As dawn broke on St. Patrick's Day, the three-man crew of the *Cascade's Gig* (another whaleboat) and I got underway and started to search for the boat from the *Preston*." Doc and his mates traveled down the bay looking for the brave men who had willingly put their lives on the line for one another.

One of Doc's crew finally spotted the whaleboat washed up on the shore of the Douglas Estate on Ocean Drive near the mouth of the harbor. As they approached, they found the bodies of Moore, Britton, and Hutchinson, "their cherry red faces frozen . . . in death." The three valiant sailors had died from exposure while searching for Kane. Their twenty-six-footer was washed ashore, miles downstream. *The Newport Daily News* later reported it was the worst storm since possibly 1938.

"George! George! Wake up! Deanie Gilmore just called to see if you were all right." Mother was standing by my bed. She told me Deanie had just heard on the radio that there had been a terrible accident aboard the *Preston*.

I was home at my parents' house in Brightwaters, Long Island, on a seventy-two-hour pass from my new ship, the USS *Abbot*, having recently transferred from the *Preston*. Both ships had been undergoing updates and repairs at the Charleston Navy Ship Yard in Boston. The *Preston* and the three other ships in her division were scheduled to leave for the West Coast to join the 7ᵗʰ Fleet for assignment in the Pacific. The *Abbot* was part of the 6ᵗʰ Fleet and would remain in the Atlantic with the three remaining destroyers in our division, operating out of Newport.

I knew instinctively that some of the men in my old division had to be involved. I spent most of the morning trying to contact the base for more information. The weather was god-awful. The *Abbot* was due to get underway from Boston early Monday. I couldn't take the chance of getting stuck in Newport and decided against my first impulse to go there immediately. Instead, I sent a telegram to the captain of the *Preston* offering my prayers and any help I could while still not knowing the details of the tragedy.

As the day progressed, the story unfolded. Sketchy details began to appear on the radio and TV. I finally got through to the office of the base commander. The duty officer confirmed the loss of four sailors and the fact that, indeed, three of the four had perished in the *Preston*'s whaleboat while trying to rescue the sailor from the *Irwin*.

Sometime in the early afternoon, the names of the sailors were released. I tuned in to the news on the radio. My heart sank as the commentator read the names: Boatswain's Mate 2, C. Robert C. Moore of Marked Tree, Arkansas; Seaman Donald Britton of Bayville, New Jersey; and Seaman Gary C. Hutchinson of Holland, Ohio. I had been their division officer.

I felt helpless. My thoughts turned to the three men aboard the whaleboat. I knew Robert Moore the best. He was a rangy, easygoing southerner, with a great sense of humor, who took his responsibilities to heart. He was popular with officers and crew alike. Robert had taken me under his wing when I reported aboard as a young, inexperienced ensign.

I thought of Britton and Hutchison—two squared-away seamen whose promise was yet to be fulfilled. The deck force, where they were stationed, is the training ground from which other activities aboard staff their personnel. They were both headed for greater responsibilities.

The whaleboat in which the men perished had been my responsibility while I was aboard. During anti-submarine warfare exercises, we used that same boat to retrieve spent torpedoes and return them to the subs. I had been the boat officer.

It had been decades since I had thought of these men and their courage. Time had not diminished the memory of their heroics. I can't help but think it's no coincidence that I ran into Harry and Doc and pieced together again the story of that night. For me, it's a stark reminder of the need to honor the sacrifice of those who give their lives for others. It's important to write their stories down and share them, to make sure people remember these four brave men, and all the men and women who so bravely serve their country.

Chapter 27

Gut-Wrenching Decision—Selling the Family Home

I sat on the ferry taking us from Orient Point, Long Island, to New London, Connecticut. From here, we would go to our new home in Essex. Somewhere deep within my mind a long-forgotten song bubbled up. I found myself thinking about the lyrics from Lerner and Loewe's "On the Street Where You Live."

For me, Woodland Drive in Brightwaters, Long Island, was *this* street. For seventy-two years of my life I lived there. 41 Woodland Drive was the home my parents had bought in

1937. After my marriage to Dorothy in 1964, we moved into 42 Woodland Drive, a cozy, charming, Belgian-style stone house with a slate roof. We lived there for more than forty-five years, raising our children.

My love affair with 42 Woodland began as a young boy. I have always referred to this bucolic fairytale "mini-castle" as my Hansel and Gretel house. My very first memory of it was on a blustery winter morning as I gazed out across the street at the proud little stone house, looking as though it could have been magically transported from high in the French Alps. A perfect plume of smoke rose from the hooded chimney centered in the middle of the peaked slate roof. The high palladium window facing out towards the street was fast disappearing in a blanket of white. The snow was swirling and drifting, blown almost horizontal by the howling east wind. The house took on a Currier and Ives-like appearance. This memory will always be with me.

My parents were both gone when we made the move to Connecticut, as was my brother Ken. As I sipped a soda at the ferry's bar, I relished the memories growing up in that wonderful neighborhood at a time when no one locked their doors. Back then, there were still open woods and fields where we built snow forts under the canopies of massive pine trees and played pick-up baseball games after school. Today, these areas are now crammed with houses and driveways full of SUVs.

The section of Woodland Drive where we lived abutted a string of five ponds with pearly white bridges and a cascade. At the turn of the nineteenth century, they were full of faux gondolas and model sailboats. Dad and Mother taught us to skate on those ponds. Ken and I became devout hockey players, playing throughout our high school and college years, accruing various broken bones and chipped teeth along the way.

Woodland Drive continues about four hundred yards west before it turns and rambles lazily north for another eighth of a mile. The western end of our section runs up next to an eighteen-hole golf course belonging to the local country club.

Before the days of mindless vandalism, the kids on the block spent many happy hours playing hide-and-seek and acting out WWII battles in the middle of the rolling course. We rode our sleds down moguls and large traps when it snowed and snuck in after sundown with clubs pilfered from our parents to try our hands at putting and driving. Today, the course is fenced and gated in tight.

41 Woodland was, for Ken and me, the base from which our lives took shape. Two wonderful, loving parents guided us wisely at every turn, passing on to us family legacies such as a love of salt water and the great outdoors, service to our country, and an abiding faith in God (though I don't seem to get to church as often as I should these days).

My brother and I shared so many things. We were best friends when we were kids, then went to the same schools, in Bay Shore and then in New England. After graduation, we served together on the USS *Abbot*. This required approval from our parents, who proudly gave us the thumbs-up. At that time we were the only brothers serving as officers together on the same ship in the entire Navy.

At every stage, we returned home to 41 Woodland. After Dorothy and I married, we purchased 42 Woodland, directly across the street from Mother and Dad.

Like Ken and me so many years before, Graham and Jenny used our house on Woodland as their home base after college as they made their way into the world and built their careers.

After our son Graham and his family moved away, there were no more babysitting duties for Dorothy and me and no more weekend soccer games or school concerts to attend. Our beloved neighbors had retired and moved to Florida. Other familiar faces had also migrated south or passed away. Houses were no longer left unlocked, and kids were no longer allowed to wait for the bus by themselves without the careful chaperoning of moms or dads holding coffee cups and checking their watches.

Still, Woodland Drive was and is still magical. It's more than just a street. Unfortunately, many kids who grew up on Long Island can no longer afford or want to return to their hometown, buy a house, and raise their children. For seniors, the expense and changes in the standard of living necessitate decisions that most of us never anticipated nor wanted to make. It's a scenario that is playing out all across the country.

After two winters of being four hours away from our beloved grandchildren, Dorothy and I made the fateful decision. We would put our beloved 42 Woodland up for sale and move to Connecticut. Pulling up roots that had been put down on Long Island eight generations before was one of the most painful experiences of my life. The dream of passing along the legacy of a life close to the Great South Bay and the Atlantic was not to be. However, Dorothy and I were very fortunate to be able to relocate near Graham and once again be near family. Although eighty-two years have passed, my recollections of life on Woodland Drive shine bright and will always be with me.

The ferry horn sounded, and I was jolted back to the present. I had spent the entire trip lost in memory. I limped off to meet Dorothy on the deck. We had a short drive ahead of us, then a joyful reunion with the grandkids to look forward to before we would begin the arduous process of unpacking and starting our new life.

The next time you hear the words and music to "On the Street Where I Live," savor the memories of the streets where you lived and raised your family. But don't be afraid to let go and move forward. Selling the family home is a life-rattling, heartbreaking affair. There's no sugarcoating it. But time marches on, and life moves on, and so can you—as Dorothy and I have.

Chapter 28

Starting Over—Part Deux

Any doubts about our decision to move to Essex, Connecticut, were put to bed a few weeks after we said our last goodbye to our beautiful home in Brightwaters, Long Island.

Our son Graham, his wife and their grandchildren—"The Fearsome Foursome"—now live right next door. Their home is at the bottom of a cul-de-sac. The lots are pie-shaped, fanning out and leading back to a stream surrounded by woods in the back. Our house is nestled between Graham's and a large wooded lot.

My office faces the cul-de-sac, which surrounds a number of fir trees and looks out over our driveway leading up to it. Dorothy came back from shopping one day and joined me in my office.

Dorothy turned around and looked out the window behind her. "George, look at this!"

I stopped typing and turned to see our daughter-in-law Paulette and five-year-old Duncan bundled up against the cold walking down their driveway. Duncan was leading their new Havanese puppy on a leash. Paulette was being pulled along by Ranger, a determined black lab. They were headed for the bus stop.

Fifteen minutes passed. Now it was my turn. "Dear, here they come!"

Ranger and Fid were now unleashed and racing for home, followed by Paulette and Duncan. Straggling behind them were Graham Jr. and Tory, weighed down by book bags. Bradley was racing to the head of the pack with his backpack in hand in full stride.

The sight of Paulette shepherding her flock with the dogs and the looks on the faces of our four grandchildren was worth every bit of the year-and-a-half-long struggle that the sale of our house entailed.

"Yes, dear, we made the right decision," I tell Dorothy. Not everyone has the opportunity to move near their kids and their grandkids when they get old. If you're one of the fortunate few who does, I strongly suggest you take it.

Chapter 29

Rosie—Old Rogue's Best Friend

I gradually eased into retirement in 1995, trying this and that until I found new interests and passions. It wasn't easy. But the true days from Hell occurred three months later when my younger brother Ken died suddenly of an undetected heart condition. His beautiful daughter Ellen had died a decade before from melanoma at the tender age of twenty-four. Ken was to be buried next to her on the grounds of the Episcopal Church in Manhasset.

The day of his funeral was hot and sunny. There was a light breeze from the northwest. The weather was fitting for an avid sailor like Ken.

Dorothy and I drove home from the ceremony in silence, numb from the day's events. I had delivered the eulogy. Little did we know that the day was far from over.

Razzie, our faithful poodle of eighteen years, wasn't at the door to greet us. He had suffered a stroke while we were away. Dorothy wrapped him in a towel, and we drove immediately to our vet. We paced and waited, and then came the terrible news. Dorothy held him when he died. I couldn't bear to.

We took Razzie home. I got the shovel from the shed and, still dressed in my funeral outfit, I buried him next to his sister Suzie. They had come to us the same day from the same kennel. Inseparable in life, they were now side by side again by the holly bush.

It was getting dark. I was bone tired and took a shower. Dorothy checked the phone messages.

There are some people, like my Dad, who say bad things come in threes. Dorothy called to me, "Dr. Smith wants you to call him in the morning." I had just taken my annual physical and assumed that I would be lectured about my weight.

Dad was right. When I called the doctor's office, it turned out not to be my weight. The problem was that my PSA was elevated. A later biopsy confirmed my fears, and my prostate would be removed in late August at Sloan Kettering.

Dorothy was still working as a nurse at our local hospital, and I was still coping with the long rehab after the prostate removal. One day just before Halloween that fall, the phone rang.

"Mr. Rider, this is the Bay Shore Animal Hospital. We know how much you and Mrs. Rider love dogs. At lunchtime today a woman working for a company headquartered at the industrial park in nearby Hauppauge came into the waiting room carrying a small black dog in her arms. The dog was in bad shape. She's so sweet. Her coat was so matted that it took two hours to cut the hair under the crust just to get her to where we could bathe her. She was very dehydrated and she is also malnourished. In addition, when the girl found her, she was tethered to a wire mesh fence by a piece of clothesline knotted to the collar. The collar was fastened too tight. The line was only long enough to allow her to seek partial refuge under a car, parked overnight at the curb. She was terrified by the thunderstorm last night. She tugged so hard that her neck bled and was still seeping blood around the collar."

Halfway through the story, I began to tear up. By the time the vet had finished, I was ready to track down the culprit and inflict bodily harm on him or her. I was practically speechless.

"Mr. Rider, this dog deserves a home, a very good home with people who will understand and love her. Your names were first up. Would you consider taking her?"

"I'm flattered. Dorothy is at work. Don't do anything till I call you back. Thanks again for thinking of us."

"Would it help if I brought her by after work so you can meet her?" the vet said.

Without hesitation I said, "Yes." The die was cast!

Our doorbell rang around 6:30 p.m. The vet came in carrying a dog with deep brown eyes. Dorothy took one look at the dog, and it was love at first sight. The poor dog was nearly bald; her coat had been trimmed almost to the skin. She was hesitant at first to wander far from where the vet was seated. She sniffed here and there, and then suddenly made a bee-line for Dorothy.

By now the dog was in Dorothy's lap. The vet teared up. Dorothy looked at me. We knew that the dog was staying. The vet departed with our thanks, but not before one last, long hug with the dog she had labored over lovingly just hours before.

We named her Rosie, after Dorothy's departed and much-missed mom. Her first night was spent on a makeshift bed in the kitchen. Every night after that she slept between us on our bed.

She was an amazing dog—the best friend and traveling companion you could ask for—and we were blessed to have her in our lives for twelve years until she passed away in her sleep just before we moved to Essex, Connecticut.

A few days after Rosie arrived, Dorothy confessed that she had bumped into the vet in the grocery store right after Razzie was put to sleep. She asked the vet to call her if any poodles became available for adoption (Rosie had a smidge of poodle and probably some cocker spaniel to boot). The call from the vet's office that day was anything but random. As usual, my wife was five steps ahead of me.

Don't ever underestimate the importance of a pet, especially as you get older. Four-legged companions never need their noses wiped, never argue with you, never ask to borrow the car "just this once," and always express their appreciation. They also never leave for college or get married and have kids. They stay and love you forever.

When my thoughts drift back to that terrible day when the world seemed to be taking aim at an invisible target sign on my back, I think of Rosie and all that she gave to me and to our family, and the world seems right again. I encourage you to rescue a shelter dog or cat. They make life so much better and aging so much more bearable.

Chapter 30

Death of a Friend—A Well-Lived Life in Retirement

My friend and former classmate Jerry Lasley called the shots all the way. Rugged and resolute with a trimmed beard and a twinkle in his eye, he looked the part of the seafarer in the old Schweppes ads from the 1950s— smiling, free, and full of high spirits. To me, Jerry was an amazing example of someone who thrived at every stage in life. He taught me that, with careful planning, retirement and your later years can truly be your best and most fulfilling.

Jerry made some smart decisions as a young man. He entered Brown University with the goal of becoming an electrical engineer. After a rough start, the dean of students politely suggested that since his performance did not match his test scores, "It would be a good idea for him to go away for a while."

He took the dean's advice and spent two years in the Army in Texas to sow his oats and straighten up. Before returning to college he married a woman he "had been chasing since the senior prom at Andover," the younger sister of a classmate. At the wedding, the brother was overheard saying, "Jesus, all I asked you to do was to take my sister to a dance, not marry her!" Marriage and the Army agreed with Jerry. He returned to college, changed his major to economics, and graduated on the dean's list.

Jerry also chose wisely with his career, starting out as a financial trainee with General Electric. He worked hard and enjoyed a stellar career, capped off as corporate comptroller at National Starch and Chemical and later Amerace. He and Joan had two children, who each in turn produced two grandchildren.

Five years after joining Amerace, and with the last college tuition paid ("the biggest raise I ever received"), Jerry retired and opened his own firm in Norwalk, Connecticut, specializing as a financial consultant to small businesses. He used to say, "I like working with real people, doing real things, people I can help."

While busy working on his business, Jerry starting another job: planning his eventual retirement. An organizational wizard, he plotted out a careful path for himself and Joan. He was more on the ball about retiring than anyone I have ever known. And his thoughtful approach paid dividends. He sold his business in 1995 and met up with the second love of his life—*Lady Blue*, a forty-eight-foot offshore yacht/fishing boat. With the first casting off of the Lasley's dream boat, the wonderful story of Jerry's well-lived retirement began.

Lady Blue was a beauty. It boasted teak interior state-rooms below deck fore and aft, each with a hot shower, and a smaller stateroom forward fitted out as a fully equipped office complete with a computer, fax machine, working desk, and file area. A roomy lounge took up part of the main deck. It was separated from a spacious galley and bar/eating space with an ice machine and large color TV set. The whole ship would have made the *QE2* envious. The navigation bridge was up deck over the main cabin. The chart table was on the port side with cushioned seats rimming the entire bridge area—perfect for navigating, viewing, and socializing. There was enough electronics gear aboard to launch the Saturn. *Lady Blue* also had serious firepower, flanked by twin 350-horsepower Cummings diesel engines with a maximum speed of 21 knots.

The maiden voyage of *Lady Blue* took Jerry and Joan to Boston and then Booth Bay Harbor, Maine, for their fortieth wedding anniversary. Afterwards, they lived aboard for a year, home ported in Watch Hill, Rhode Island. Heading off another frigid New England winter, *Lady Blue* headed south the next fall in search of a new home base. Jerry and Joan along with their cat Sinbad nosed in and out of several Florida locations, finally deciding on Punta Gorda as the final destination. They bought a condo in eyeshot of their seagoing home and began their new life, becoming active in the local community, with their children and grandchildren stopping by for frequent visits.

While the rest of our buddies—including and especially me—seemed to struggle to find our footing after retiring, Jerry seemed to hit his stride. I'm not sure if that was because of his meticulous planning, or simply because Jerry was always someone totally comfortable in his own skin. He just had the gift to continually blossom wherever he was planted—on land or at sea.

Fast forward to our fiftieth Andover reunion in June 2001. Our class was not particularly motivated, and we were in need of a jumpstart. The fiftieth is a milestone for everyone in or near retirement. For those attending, it's a chance to be with old friends and relive parts of our youth. For the institution, it's an opportunity to shine a light on the graduates' accomplishments and the school's progress. If it's a private school, it's also an opportunity to raise money from the alumni exuberance.

I have always taken old friendships seriously. I believe wholeheartedly that maintaining the bonds with the people with whom you grew up and went to school is essential to a full and happy life, so I am always enthusiastic about any kind of reunion. For our fiftieth, I joined forces with a merry band of pranksters. But to rally the troops and get people motivated to come back for the day, we needed more help.

We decided to produce a fat class reunion book, as some classes had done before us, complete with the biographies, photos, and "greatest hits" of each class member. It became obvious that this task would be more than one person could handle. But we knew exactly who to call to backstop: Jerry, our organizational wonder boy and chief cheerleader.

The trouble was, how to catch up with him? He and Joan had become world-class travelers. They had planned and were about to embark on the trip of a lifetime. They ordered charts for a six thousand-mile, six-month odyssey, weighing anchor and heading north up and down the Eastern seaboard.

All the while, I had been trying to track him down by phone to tell him, "Jerry, I need a favor!" I could barely walk down the street on my arthritic legs, and Jerry was a nonstop ball of energy, darting from harbor to harbor.

When I finally reached Jerry by phone, we agreed to meet up. Jerry and Joan put in on the north shore of Long Island and picked Dorothy and me up for a visit. We boarded *Lady Blue* and were soon on the Long Island Sound heading for the East River. We rounded the tip of Manhattan and headed down past Ellis Island and around the Statue of Liberty. We continued north and swung in for a close look at the *Intrepid* and the other ships at the museum pier. We sailed under the George Washington Bridge, then the Tappan Zee, and tied up at the Tarrytown Marina for the night.

Over dinner, the years dissolved, and Jerry and I were teenagers again. That's when I enlisted him to join in with the planning of our reunion.

I had boarded *Lady Blue* ostensibly to ask Jerry for his help, but he had helped me. I had just retired the year before and was still feeling lost and unmoored. Jerry showed me how to set a clear course and sail for it.

After our visit, *Lady Blue* headed north in earnest. As Jerry and Joan made their long voyage, he was busy on board developing ideas for our book, painstakingly designing a survey of classmates about their lives, and enlisting others to help. Joan, ever the ideal first mate, became his co-editor.

In late September, *Lady Blue* returned to Punta Gorda having completed 5,628 miles in five months. Family and friends lined the dock with balloons and welcome home signs. Horns sounded, whistles blew, hands waved up and down.

Jerry's friends lived their odyssey vicariously through their phone calls, emails, and reports. Their exploits included bicycle trips inland to visit local harbors, explorations by sea aboard their inflatable outboard, and sipping merlot at anchor while watching the sunset. Even after returning from their journey, Jerry and Joan stayed busy. They dove into the job of publishing the reunion book and once again involved themselves in their on-land community. They spent the better part of a year typing, editing, and finally producing a gorgeous, glossy, 250-page book that became the lynchpin of our class get-together and a treasured memory for many. The Lasleys sailed *Lady Blue* north to Massachusetts for the reunion, which was an outstanding success that reconnected old friends and raised more than five million dollars for the school, much of it going to scholarships for deserving young students.

Several years later, Jerry was stricken with stomach cancer. An operation to remove the tumor was scheduled for early September. He took a dramatic turn for the worse during the summer of 2004, just prior to Hurricane Ivan. With Joan by his side, he was medevaced from Florida to Memorial Sloan-Kettering Cancer Center in New York. Dorothy and I visited him there. There was something surreal about discussing Jerry's wishes with Joan, as we stood in the corridor outside his room while he was fighting to stay alive. She told us his fondest hope: "I want to go home to look out on the water again."

Jerry, Joan, and Sinbad flew back to Punta Gouda in mid-September. Friends had prepared for their return. Jerry's final wish was granted. Home in his own bed, he passed away one afternoon, looking out at the water with Joan by his side. Jerry's love of family, the sea, and his many lifelong friends were evident throughout his last days.

Jerry had dreams and lived them to the fullest. *Lady Blue* was his vehicle and Joan his beloved co-pilot. No place he wanted to go was inaccessible. He planned and executed with precision, and he accomplished his goals and then some. The love for his family, his ability to achieve and give back, and his extraordinary talent at appreciating life and accepting his fate while still fighting are lessons for us all.

I learned from Jerry not to put off doing those things that matter, no matter how tired or achy or grumpy you may feel. Do them while you can, and record the events as they unfold. The ship's log of *Lady Blue* that Jerry painstakingly kept will be savored and remembered by his family and friends forever. It is a tribute to a life well-lived and a man well-loved. Jerry was the perfect example of how to retire. He was a captain in command of his ship right through to the end.

Chapter 31

Ships That Pass in the Day—Small Town Smiles

One of my biggest gripes about how much the world is changing (and trust me, as an old rogue, I have many) is the demise of old-fashioned small town living.

Back in my day (cue to one of my grandchildren to yawn), families lived in small towns for generations. Their kids grew up together and stayed tight all of their lives. I was lucky enough to live in the same hometown for more than seventy years and raise my kids there. While Dorothy and I moved to Connecticut in our late seventies to be closer to our kids, my heart will always reside in my hometown. Luckily, even though we no longer live there, the friendships we had and the bonds we shared have continued to endure. In fact, no matter where we travel, we always seem to find a connection to someone there. My favorite "hometown boy" story took place back in my Navy days, in the unlikely location of the South Atlantic.

At sea aboard the USS *Abbot* during the late summer of 1956, we were steaming in formation with the carrier USS *Antietam*, several replenishment ships, twelve destroyers, and four destroyer escorts, all involved in a hunter-killer (HUK) exercise. Our task was to protect the supply ships from four prowling submarines and at the same time act as a screen for the *Antietam's* flight operations in support of the anti-submarine warfare mission.

Ominous rumblings in the Middle East portended an uncertain future. As Nasser was sword-rattling, the exercises took on an added significance. (In fact, three months later, we would find ourselves in the eastern Mediterranean patrolling. Nasser had sealed off the Suez Canal, blown up several ships, and blocked off all traffic.)

At breakfast a week into the exercise, our captain—Commander W. W. DeVenter (WWD), a much-decorated Annapolis graduate—announced to me in the wardroom, "Red, report to the bridge at noon. You're going to take us alongside the *Antietam* to fuel."

I had turned twenty-four that May and was soon to be promoted from ensign to lieutenant junior grade. My heart started to pound. I was the youngest of three ensigns and anxious in more than one way. Fueling at sea is a tricky and exact procedure that demands timing, discipline, and teamwork. From the time the first line is received until you disengage, chances for dangerous errors are ever present.

I thought of my father, a former British Navy officer, and my grandfather, a devoted bayman, who dreamed of going to sea but was turned down by Annapolis because of poor eyesight. The sea was in our blood. How proud Dad and Gramp would be to know of my pending assignment.

I reported to the bridge before noon to check our course, speed, and bearing to the *Antietam*. I was keyed up like a rookie hockey player in his first shift waiting for the puck to drop.

We were steaming ahead of the carrier, off to starboard, as part of an eight-destroyer screen. One of the other destroyers had just finished fueling and was en route back to the screen as a second destroyer maneuvered into place. It was time for us "to get in line" at the pump.

"Right full rudder, make turns for fifteen knots, come to course 140 degrees," I stammered. The butterflies exited my stomach. We circled back and around astern to starboard of the *Antietam*, assuming a parallel course and speed and in line with the destroyer fueling ahead of us.

Our turn came. I gave orders to increase speed, and we settled into place alongside the *Antietam*. Our deck force was led by two outstanding first class boatswain's mates. Receiving and connecting the fuel hose and the high-line, which was used for exchanging mail, films, and occasional goodies like fresh ice cream, were routines they handled with skill and enthusiasm. The fuel began flowing and the high-line transfers were taking place at a fast pace.

I was so preoccupied with our positioning and the transfers taking place that I failed to notice the activity on the carrier's bridge several stories above us. To my astonishment, their OOD hollered down through his bullhorn, "George Rider."

I looked up to see John Cochrane, a neighbor of ours from Brightwaters, Long Island. My cap was off, and my red hair helped him make the identification. John was an Annapolis graduate and a role model to many of us facing military service. Dad and Gramp followed his career closely. In fact, our whole town did.

I called to the petty officer of the watch. "Get my brother up here."

Kenny appeared. We hollered and waved up to John with our caps off (Kenny also had red hair). John's captain shouted at him, "What's going on down there on that destroyer?"

"Those redheads are brothers. They're friends of mine from my hometown. They are a little nuts."

We topped off and began to disengage. The *Antietam's* band serenaded us from the flight deck. The last two numbers played were "The Navy Hymn" and "Anchors Away." The memory still gives me goose bumps. I ordered course and speed changes to take us back to our position in the screen and received a "well done" from Captain WWD, who never moved from his chair on the bridge. The carrier graded us on the fueling exercise. We received top marks, no doubt with an assist from John.

At the conclusion of the operation, we proceed to the Mayport Naval Station in Jacksonville, Florida. The *Antietam* was already in port. Ken and I wasted no time looking up Lieutenant John, who immediately suggested a "debriefing" at the officers club. The two Ensigns Rider were treated to several adult beverages and the company of our hometown pal.

Both John and I eventually married and settled in our hometown and raised our families. Before we moved to Connecticut, Dorothy and I used to see a lot of John and his wife Betty. When our cars passed in town or our boats passed on the bay, I'd think about Ken and John and that day in the South Atlantic fifty years ago. Then I'd smile and tip my cap. You can't beat small town living.

Chapter 32

Frozen Nose—The Way Sports Used to Be

God bless the NHL for resurrecting outdoor hockey! I was sitting in my den on New Year's Day four years ago and watching the clock approach game time for the Boston Bruins vs. the Philadelphia Flyers at Fenway Park's temporary outdoor rink constructed for the game.

"Kids!" I screamed to my grandchildren in the next room. "Come here quick and let me show you how sports are *supposed* to be played." My mind raced back to a cold day on February 14, 1951, which was the day of the annual grudge match between rivals Andover and Exeter.

Saturday's morning English class seemed like it lasted a week. I ate nothing at lunch. We dressed in the old Borden Gym. Pulling my game jersey over my shoulder and elbow pads was never easy. It was the biggest game of my life, and as captain, I would also be part of the dedication ceremony for the new artificial outdoor rink—the first of its kind for a private school. Reporters observed our practices all week. My parents had arrived the day before to show their support. Brother Ken and I ate steak dinners with them at the Andover Inn that night.

Coach Leavitt addressed us in the locker room on game day. I added a few words. We banged sticks on the locker room floor. I led the team to the gym's side door. I stepped out with my heart pounding.

To get to the rink, we had to go down an incline, across a road, and down again. The crowd spotted us and began to cheer. It was goose bump time! My first few breaths froze the hairs in my nose. You could chin yourself on the exhales.

Mom and Dad were bundled against the cold, standing behind the boards on the near blue line. We took the ice for the warm-up. Guests at the pre-dedication luncheon included the *Boston Globe's* John Ahern, the *Boston Post's* Warren (Doc) Mooney, reporter/cartoonist Fred Cole from the *Boston Herald*, WBZ sports announcer "Bump Hadley," Headmaster John Kemper, Exeter Headmaster William Saltonstall, alumni, friends, and other dignitaries. For a teenager, the stakes couldn't get any higher.

John Ahern wrote, "The dedication of the Sumner Smith Rink took place at center ice." The weather conditions were severe. School officials and Referee Cleary were discussing canceling the game. Bill Saltonstall grabbed a broom and headed for center ice. John Kemper quickly followed. Students from both Andover and Exeter all grabbed brooms. The ice was cleared. The game was on. Referee Cleary dropped the puck. The ice was hard. You could hear the skates cutting into it. The pace was fast. Midway through the first period,

I checked the Exeter captain. He hooked his blade and fell awkwardly onto the ice, with a broken leg. At eleven minutes into the period, my classmate Hi Upson scored the first goal on passes from Charlie Pratt and Bill Duffy.

Three minutes into the second period, I scored the only goal of my career on a pass from Duffy. In short order, he scored himself, followed by teammates Ed Carey and George Scragg.

The third period was scoreless. A distinct underdog, we had done the unthinkable: We shut out our archrival 5-0, adding an explanation point to the dedication of the rink.

NBC's announcer interrupted my memories of that game. I looked up briefly, then glanced at the cold day outside and began to daydream again. On my desk is the puck with which I scored my goal. I fished it out of the net and skated it over to Dad. He later carved out enough hard rubber from the center of it to countersink an 1888 silver dollar in the center of it.

I'm sure that many old hockey players tuning in to see the Bruins and Flyers make the long walk from Fenway's locker rooms to the outdoor rink found themselves hearkening back to their own days of glory.

The next time you walk outside on a blustery, cold day, think of what hockey used to be. Thanks again, NHL, for the trip back in time.

Chapter 33

The USS *Michael Murphy* (DDG-112) Comes of Age—Honoring a Hero from the War in Afghanistan

A s I've mentioned, one of the biggest joys in being a writer is the chance to tell the story of true heroes. There is no one I can think of in recent history who was more courageous than a young man named Michael Murphy when he selflessly gave up his life in Afghanistan to protect his brothers in arms. Murphy's story and the story of his fellow Navy SEALs in Operation Red Wings was told in the bestselling book and recent blockbuster movie *Lone Survivor*. Under attack, he exposed himself to enemy fire in order to get a better signal while radioing for help for his fellow SEALs, and though mortally wounded, he somehow found the strength to end his final transmission with the words "thank you."

After learning more about him, I wrote several pieces in his honor, which were published in *The Tin Can Sailors*, the publication of the National Association of Destroyer Veterans, and had the great privilege of meeting his wonderful parents and attending the commissioning of a Navy destroyer named in his honor.

The program was set to begin on the morning of October 6, 2012. Michael's dad helped arrange for our tickets. I drove from Essex to New York City with my daughter Jenny to meet up with my friend Harry Flynn and a few of my *Abbot* shipmates.

Two years beforehand, I had first spotted the ship during a Navy reunion tour in Portland, Maine, at the Bath Iron Works. Dorothy pointed to the red-leaded stern section of the destroyer with "Michael Murphy" stenciled on her transom. I had heard of Michael's extraordinary story—he had grown up twenty miles from our home on Long Island—but at that time I was unaware a ship was being named in his honor. I welled up.

A year later, my shipmates and our families attended the christening of the destroyer in Bath. Members of the Navy SEALs, Army Night Stalkers, New York Fire Department, New York Police Department, and first responders all arrived on a crisp Maine morning. At the ceremony, Michael's father paid tribute to his son, sharing that it was Michael's birthday that day and movingly recounting the incident in which he lost his life.

Michael's mother read the names of all nineteen who died that day, then moved to a platform by the bow and broke the champagne bottle on the second try. She paused, looked skyward, and said, "Happy Birthday, Baby." The band played and confetti streamed.

Fast-forward to the ship's commissioning at Pier 88 in New York City. The fast-paced program began at 10:00 a.m. Commander Corey J. Turner, Executive Officer announced honored guests. Two Navy jets roared overhead followed by three Navy SEALs parachuting from a helicopter and landing on the roof of the pier.

Commander Shultz escorted Senator Schumer aboard. Honors were rendered. The youngest member of the ship's company, Seaman Recruit Stephen Martinez, sang the National Anthem.

Commander Turner directed attention to the large, tattered American flag fastened to the pier wall behind us, the largest to survive 9/11. Members of the New York City Fire Department had lovingly restored it.

The guests were announced and seated, led by Michael's brother and their father. The colors were retired.

Monsignor Robert Coyle, now a retired lieutenant commander, was both the casualty officer the night Michael went missing on June 28, 2005, and the celebrant at Michael's mass at our Lady of Carmel Church in Patchogue on July 13, 2005. He summed up Michael's deeds as such: "In the name of the Lord, no greater love hath any man than to lay down his life for his friends."

The USS *Michael Murphy* is 510 feet in length, 59 feet wide, draws 31 feet, weighs 9,200 tons, and cost $1.1 billion. She was decked out in signal flags and red, white, and blue bunting aboard and on the gangways fore and aft, which included a handsome picture of Michael, the ship's coat of arms, and the ship's motto, "Lead the Fight."

Mayor Michael Bloomberg spoke, recalling Michael's bond with the New York City Fire Department. It began with his childhood friend and fellow lifeguard, whose fireman uncle perished on 9/11. Their bond grew closer as they grew older. Michael had asked for twenty-five patches from the New York City Fire Fighters Engine Company 53/ Ladder Company 43, headquartered in Spanish Harlem ("El Barrio's Bravest"), to be distributed to his team before deploying to Afghanistan. Michael wore his patch on every mission, including the one in which he fell. The patch was cut from his uniform and returned to the fire house.

The Bath Iron Works President Jeffrey Geiger spoke of the 5,200 dedicated workers who built the *Murphy*. Their cry as they labored to complete her for his May birthday was, "Do it for Murph!" He spoke of Michael's "spirit and strength that runs deep into the plates."

Admiral Bill McCraven, Commander of Joint Special Operations Command, called for applause for all the Gold Star moms and dads, directing his attention to Michael's parents. He stressed the meaning of "team" and how it applies in his command. Teammates "live together, fight together, and sometimes die together." He spoke of Michael's raw courage in the face of death, adding how proud he was to see the *Murphy* ride into battle again.

Congressman Peter King spoke of Michael's class and dignity, observing that with one look at his parents, you knew why Michael did what he did! He extolled Michael's unbridled courage.

Senator Charles Schumer stressed that Michael represented the best of America and Long Island. As an eighth-grader, Michael had come to the aid of a special needs student being harassed by a group of teenagers. He chased another group that tormented a homeless man and helped pick up empty cans the kids had heartlessly snatched from him. Even as a boy, Michael displayed strength, courage, and humility.

Admiral Jonathan W. Greenert, Chief of Naval Operations, called New York a Navy town. He commented on the hospitality displayed yearly to the Navy during Fleet Week and referred to the *Michael Murphy* as the center of our fleet. He repeated her motto "Lead the Fight," then introduced the seventy-fifth Secretary of the Navy, Ray Mabus.

Ray Mabus quoted Ecclesiastes: "To everything there is a season, time for every purpose under heaven. Michael's time was far too short; it's how well he used the time given him." As recounted, Michael's nickname growing up was the "protector." That was also true of his SEAL team. He retold the story of Michael's valor. Michael's favorite book, *Gates of Fire* by Steven Pressfield, recounts the Battle of Thermopolis. The Spartans were greatly outnumbered, but their courage inspired Mabus's observation that Michael's parents had raised a man "whose action truly transcends itself and touches the sublime."

At the end of his remarks, Mabus joined Captain Shultz at the podium for the formalities that would officially place the USS *Michael Murphy* in commission. Commander Shultz, captain of the *Murphy*, ordered the colors hoisted, followed by the commission pennant.

Shultz then ordered the executive officer to set the watch. The OOD received a long glass offered by Michael's brother and father in accordance with Navy tradition as the boatswain piped.

Command Master Chief Matthew Danforth escorted Michael's mother to the podium. Captain Shultz handed her the mike, and in a strong voice, she ordered, "Officers and crew of the USS *Michael Murphy*, man your ship and bring her to life!" The band played "Anchors Aweigh" as the crew, standing behind the seated guests, broke in the middle and double-timed it to the gangways fore and aft, and then fanned out, manning the rails and open spaces from the main deck to the bridge. The ship's horn sounded one long blast.

Captain Shultz ordered the Secretary of the Navy's flag to be hoisted and then reported for duty to the squadron commander. He began his talk by stressing unity aboard. "All together, all in one!"

He read the names of all nineteen of the SEALs and Night Stalkers who perished in Operation Red Wings. He added that the crew proudly carries on the legacy of Michael and his teammates, and that he would be proud to take the ship into battle against anyone.

Captain Shultz then asked Michael's mother to help him do something that no other ship does. Together they stood while he pointed skyward and shouted, "Hooyah, Michael Murphy!" The crew and the thousands in the audience answered in unison, "Hooyah, Michael Murphy!" This was the battle cry of the Navy SEALs.

At one point during the ceremony, a cannon fired a multiple gun salute, and charges from three torpedo tubes were fired later in the program. The unforgettable sight of Navy SEAL Marcus Luttrell, the lone survivor of Operation Red Wings, standing on the pier surrounded by the honor guard all added to the solemnity of the celebration.

Monsignor Coyle blessed the crew of the *Michael Murphy* and Michael's family. "Lord bless this mighty ship and guard her going forth."

The *Michael Murphy* was conceived, born, and christened in Bath. She came of age at Pier 88 in New York. God bless her as she takes her place in the Pacific Fleet. All ahead flank!

Chapter 34

True Courage—Captain Thomas Hudner

Not only has writing become a wonderful hobby in retirement, it's also opened up new worlds for me, as I research and write down not just my own stories, but also the stories of friends, loved ones, and people I admire and hold in awe. Captain Thomas Hudner is a shining example of the latter.

The Greatest Generation has, and always will be, an inspiration to me. The selfless dedication, bravery, and leadership they provided will always be a standard to which future generations aspire. A man named Thomas Hudner epitomizes the very best of these courageous men and women. I've had the great fortune of meeting and getting to know him over the years. I have the great fortune now of telling his story.

On May 7, 2012, Secretary of the Navy Ray Maybus announced the next Arleigh Burns-class destroyer would be named USS *Thomas Hudner* for the Medal of Honor recipient Lieutenant Junior Grade Thomas Hudner. He was awarded the Medal by President Harry S. Truman in April 1951 for his valiant actions trying to save the life of his wingman, Ensign Jesse L. Brown, during the Battle of Chosin Reservoir.

Tom is the oldest surviving recipient of the Medal of Honor, one of 145 awarded from that war, and the only one awarded to a Naval aviator during that period.

As the Medal of Honor Citation noted, "For conspicuous gallantry and intrepidity at the risk of his life above and beyond the call of duty in attempting to rescue a squadron mate forced down behind enemy lines, struck by enemy fire. Lt. J.G. Hudner risked his life to save the injured flier trapped alive in the burning wreckage."

What an amazing story this is. After Jesse's plane was shot down, Hudner made a courageous rescue attempt, bringing his plane down skillfully in a wheels-up landing on the rough, mountainous terrain in the presence of enemy troops. When he reached the crashed plane, Hudner packed snow into the fuselage with his bare hands to keep the flames away and struggled to extricate the trapped pilot inside, but he could not pull him out. Hudner returned to his plane and requested a helicopter with an axe and fire extinguisher, then remained on-site in the sub-freezing cold and in danger from the enemy. With the help of the helicopter pilot, Hudner once again battled against the cold and flames to try to rescue the first pilot, who tragically did not survive. According to the citation, "Lt. J.G. Thomas Hudner's exceptionally valiant action and selfless devotion to a shipmate sustain and enhance the highest traditions of the U.S. Naval Service."

The man Tom tried so courageously to save—Jesse Brown—was honored in 1973 with the commissioning of the Knox-class frigate USS *Jesse L. Brown*, the first ship named in honor of an African-American serviceman. Tom, who retired soon after as captain after twenty-seven years of service, joined Jesse's widow Daisy and daughter Pamela for the commissioning and gave a dedication.

Now, it was Tom's turn to be honored with a ship bearing his name. The centuries-old tradition—a triad that brings a ship to life—begins with the keel-laying, followed by the christening, culminating with the commissioning, which marks the entrance of a man-of-war into the Naval Forces of our nation. In addition to the destroyer named for him, the U.S. Postal Service recently struck a stamp in his honor.

What a remarkable generation. What a remarkable man.

Chapter 35

Bedtime for 25 Shell Walk—As Seasons Come and Seasons Go...

2 5 Shell Walk. This is the address of our rambling beach cottage set back from the Great South Bay in a nest of bulrushes and bayberry bushes. It was built in 1939 by the head of our family to replace the original bungalow, which had been washed out to sea in the 1938 hurricane.

There is an aura about the place. The knotty pine interior lends a certain majesty to it. It has a particular smell—a mix of mildew, mothballs, old books, and suntan lotion, no matter the season. My grandfather's favorite pastime was carving (the perfect hobby for a retired surgeon), so more than one hundred wooden ducks and geese in mid-flight dot the south wall of the living room. The chandelier, a large ship's lamp, was one of only a few treasures to survive the 1938 hurricane. The lantern was retrieved a year later from the bay's bottom by a clammer and returned to his grateful friend and doctor. (Gramp tended to many baymen over the years.)

Other distinctive items are the lamps made of kedge anchors and water kegs, powder horns, arrowheads, and a skin from a six-foot-long rattlesnake that was shot by Gramp on safari (a "don't touch" no-no for the little ones). Sword and sailfish bills hang over the doors. There are a dozen watercolor scenes of French shell fisherman, pre-World War II menu covers from the famous Paris restaurant Pruniers, and a collection of bottles and jars retrieved from the beach and bay bottom, some dating back to the late 1800s. The andirons in the large stone fireplace sport Gramp's initials. The fire screen sports a sailing ship cut from a sheet of copper. It creates a majestic and imposing silhouette when the fire is blazing.

To me, 25 Shell is a temple to timelessness. I'm in my eighties now. Each fall, I close the house for the winter. In recent years, the ritual seems to take longer and longer, while somehow the memories grow sharper. This is one of the many paradoxes of growing older.

As the oldest surviving member of the family, I feel a particular responsibility to preserve this house, its contents, and above all the memories for future generations.

Gramp named the cottage "La Casa Del Perro," which means doghouse in Spanish and hearkens back to the time when the original house was built as a fishing and hunting shack, and the place where the men in the family were banished for their various misdeeds. "La Casa" is now referred to as the "Old House."

The name is also fitting because it has been the address of preference for fourteen black Labradors, four poodles, one

Havenese, ten cats, several English setters, and our dearly departed Rosie. Currently, my son's lab and feisty Havenese, as well as my daughter's dog, all call "La Casa Del Perro" home for part of the season.

After the 1938 hurricane, Gramp rebuilt with what little remained of the original house—a wheelbarrow load of stones left over from the fireplace. At the time, it was the only structure on a large tract of land with an uninterrupted view of the bay. He had the house canted to provide better views of the sunsets. Today, the house sits behind three modern bay-front cottages owned by my two cousins and me.

Gramp had two daughters. One, my mother, was a spirited debutante renowned for being gently nudged out of several tony girls' boarding schools in the Northeast. Her ability to swim across the six-mile-wide bay without getting winded and her devotion to our pack of black labs is legendary. She and Dad, a Brit, had two sons, me and Ken. Mom's younger sister Elinor also produced two sons. The four of us boys, in turn, have produced twenty grandchildren, all of whom were born with salt water in their veins, all of whom return each year, a little taller, with a little less time to chat and fish with their granddads.

Each fall, I put off the inevitable and linger here despite the family's chiding. Others volunteer to help, albeit on their timetables, which are much busier than my own now that I've retired. The fault is mine for delaying the process, for feeling relieved when everyone else ducks out. I've become methodical—a euphemism for unreasonable, according to my critics. A place for everything and everything in its place is my thinking. Plus, I like the time alone, just the house and me.

My brother Ken and I had a magical childhood here that included swimming with Mom and Dad, crabbing, snapper fishing, surf casting, lifeguarding, bodysurfing, feasting on grilled steaks and corn-on-the-cob (Long Island, of course). I have so many wonderful memories of row boats, sunfish, skiffs, water skiing, northeast squalls, cigar clouds, thunder, lightning, full moons, poison ivy, splinters, sunburn, and the universal I-don't-want-to-go-to-bed-yet moments.

Like an old bear heading off for hibernation, one by one I check off items from the list: beds stripped; blankets folded and mothballed; deck furniture, beach chairs, umbrellas stacked and stowed; refrigerator emptied and unplugged; windows locked and shades drawn. Finally, there's quiet.

The sights and sounds and activities of the past summer become memories to be replayed and added to the future. "Poppy, where's my crab trap?" one of my grandkids will ask me. Graham Jr., Brad, and Tory run everywhere like wind-up toys. Duncan, the baby, grows bigger by the minute. I hear happy chatter from the kitchen where Dorothy, Jenny, and Paulette cook together. There are the familiar smells of coffee, orange slices, and bacon.

One memory triggers others. I think about Graham and Jenny here at this house as chubby toddlers. I remember Dad waking my brother and me each morning at dawn and calling us to attention as we raised the American and UK flags. Sunday suppers were occasionally interrupted by a knock on the door, and the grownups would suddenly transform the dining room table into an operating table while my grandfather readied himself at the kitchen sink to treat an injured fisherman. I remember black-out shades hanging on the windows in the early days of the war, and good-bye dinners for young ones heading off to the service, including me.

Suddenly I snap back to reality. It's getting cold. It's time to go. I flip the master switch. The electricity is off. I lock the door and then struggle with my new cell phone. "It's me, dear. I'm heading home now."

Dorothy replies, "Hurry. It's starting to get dark."

I board our little skiff, *The Rough Riders*, to cross the bay and fetch the car for the drive home to Connecticut for the winter. Twenty-five Shell has been put to bed for another season. There's a feeling of satisfaction but with it a certain melancholy. I watch over my shoulder as 25 Shell's roof disappears, slipping away in my wake. Only five months to go, and then there'll be a new season. I'll be here, God willing, the family memory keeper, keeping up his watch. Until then, I'm heading back home—to my wife Dorothy and family, to my favorite bar stool at the Black Seal (once a rogue, always a rogue), and to my writing. Fair winds and following seas.

Epilogue

Get Out There and Enjoy Every Day!

To this day, writing remains challenging for me, but also more fulfilling with each new chapter. My hope is that my journey has been and continues to be worth sharing because my experience is similar to anyone who is struggling to accept—but not to give in—to aging. If you think of experience and wisdom as assets, then getting older is an abundance of riches. We are the lucky ones, you and I, full of memories to unpack and savor on rainy days, but still full of life and passion, ready and raring to go (as soon as the arthritis meds kick in each morning).

No one lives forever. The trick is to stay out of heaven for as long as possible. Getting there is half the fun. The lessons I've learned are these: Live in the present. Don't dwell on the past, but do record your memories for your friends, kids, and grandkids, and for posterity. And always look to the future. There's always more fun to be had—you just have to go out and find it!

Try facing aft on a boat or ship. Stare at the wake and let your mind wander. There you are looking back while still moving forward. You'll never know when you'll tie up your boat for the last time.

My parents and family members before them exited with too many stories left untold. I want to leave as many as possible for my family to sift through and take with them on their way. I hope all those reading this take the time to do so as well. It's well worth it. It's your gift to all those who are also dealing with aging—and all those who come after you. It's your legacy.

The Rogue's Road to Retirement may have its share of bumps along the way, but the path ahead can be full of glorious adventures (and misadventures) and some damned good fun. You just have to go for it. Drive on, fellow rogues, drive on!

Letter from the Skipper

A prize possession! Had I not broken my leg I would have stayed in. Two of the best years of my life!

U.S.S. ABBOT (DD-629)
Care of Fleet Post Office
New York, New York

January 8, 1958

Miss Evelyn Richards
Personnel Relations Department
Bankers Trust Company
16 Wall Street
New York, New York

Dear Miss Richards,

I am given to understand that Mr. George S. K. Rider is applying for a position with Bankers Trust.

Mr. Rider served under me as a Lieutenant (junior grade) from April 1956 until January 1957 at which time he broke a leg and left my command for hospitalization. However, I have visited Mr. Rider several times since January 1957 and I have remained in touch with him up to the present, due to the fact that his brother Kenneth is now serving aboard the Abbot as an Ensign in the Engineering Department. Furthermore I have known their Parents and Grandfather since 1956.

I find George Rider to be of very high character, moderate habits and completely reliable. One finds him to be a very likable person and a person whose company one enjoys. I have given George Rider a number of responsible duties including such difficult tasks as controlling gun batteries, ship handling during fueling preparations in violent Atlantic storms and docking the ship. In those duties I found him to be of great mental and physical courage who is completely reliable. One should understand that it is certainly not everyone who is an officer in the Navy that I would entrust to those duties. Rather the person must be an all up First Class individual who is a good leader and whose ability to give orders and run things is unquestioned. Finally when one recommends a man he should comment on his general industriousness, devotion to a job and his ability to learn new techniques. In all of these, I find Mr. Rider outstanding.

It is your good fortune that Mr. Rider chose your firm. The Navy regrets his departure and would welcome him back. And I personally would be there to greet him.

Sincerely Yours,

W. W. Deventer, Commander, U.S. Navy

ACKNOWLEDGMENTS

I have had good fortune every step of the way in writing this book. My daughter, Jenny, saw something early in my writing and pushed me to apply for the Southampton Writers Conference. Five times I returned. Courses with Roger Rosenblatt, Frank McCourt, Matt Klam, and Melissa Bank helped me to develop, and the guidance of Bob Reeves, Lou Ann Walker, Carla Caglioti, and Adrienne Unger was invaluable. David Friend, Nancy Paulsen, David McCullough, Nancy Reardon, and Tom Flynn offered advice and encouragement.

I took writing classes with Cindy Dale at the Bay Shore, L.I., YMCA, and had articles printed by Susan Bela, founder, publisher, and editor-in-chief, of the Great South Bay Magazine; Terry Miller, editor and director, The Tin Can Sailor; Lou Ann Walker, editor-in-chief of The Southampton Review; Sally Holm and Jill Clerkin, past and current editors of Andover, the Magazine of Phillips Academy; Charlie Dean, editor, and the staff of the Blue Guidon, The Newsletter of Andover and the Military; Liz Finnegan, editor of The Islip Bulletin; Connecticut's Shore Line Times, and Walt Baranger, senior editor at The New York Times, and founder and editor of the USS Abbot (DD-629)'s website. In addition I had the good fortunate to participate in the "Voices in the Bookstore" program run by Forrest Stone at R. J. Julia's, the fabulous bookstore in Madison, CT.

Also special thanks to Jay Cassell and Nicole Frail at Skyhorse Publishing, my talented editor Holly Rubino, and a special shout out to daughter Jenny who met my terrific agent Anna Termine at Gather, a charming gift shop owned by Deanna Pinette in Ivoryton, CT, also home to Essex Books and its owner, Susan McCann. Without Jenny and Anna this book would never have come to life.

Additional thanks go to all the friends and colleagues who have read my stories and cheered me on: Doug, Jerry, Heather, George, Gretchen, Tracy, Holly, Doc, Nicole, Dawn, Bob, Winnie, Frank, Cathy, Tom, Joy, Chris, JP, Donna, Stan, Laurie, Matt, Peter, Richard, Channing, Billy, Shelly, Ken, Lynn, Alexandra, Amy, Dana, Sue, Connie, Dan, Ted, Jenny, Rich, Camille, Sue, Pat, Brenda, Brian, Moira, Marti, Trish, Harry, Harrison, John, Ron, Bill, Kappy, Art, Nobu, Steve, Gene, Jane, Joda, Aisha, Kelila, Raquel, Brittany, Jemel, Nayab, Mary, Nicky, Barbara, Donna, Christine, Rob, Kit, Maxine, Eric, Shelby, Joan, Dulaney, Alex, David, Ed, Muriel, Abby, Tony, Corky, Merwin, Jill, Janet, Mike, Sherl, Stu, Amy, Mark, Joan, Jane, Gus, and Don.

Finally, my love and thanks to my amazing family—wife Dorothy; son Graham, daughter-in-law Paulette, and their all-star kids Graham Jr., Bradley, Victoria, and Duncan; daughter Jenny and son-in-law Bill; the rest of the Rider, Crawford, Anderson, Furgueson, and Eiden clans; and our pack of four-leggeds, Ladybug, Marybeth, Ranger, and Fid. Never has a rogue been so lucky.